NATALIE MACMASTER

I Have a Love Story

MacIntyre Purcell Publishing Inc.

MacIntyre Purcell Publishing Inc.
232 Fairmont Road
Cloverville, Nova Scotia
B2G 2K9
(902) 640-3350
www.macintyrepurcell.com
info@macintyrepurcell.com

Printed and bound in Canada by Friesens

Cover and interior design: Gwen North

ISBN: 978-1-77276-191-7

Library and Archives Canada Cataloguing in Publication

Title: I Have a Love Story / Natalie MacMaster.
Names: MacMaster, Natalie, author.
Identifiers: Canadiana 20250192640 | ISBN 9781772761917 (hardcover)
Subjects: LCSH: MacMaster, Natalie. | LCSH: Fiddlers—Nova Scotia—Cape Breton Island—Biography. | LCGFT: Autobiographies.
Classification: LCC ML418.M172 A3 2025 | DDC 787.2/16291607169—dc23

Canada Council for the Arts Conseil des Arts du Canada

MacIntyre Purcell Publishing Inc. would like to acknowledge the financial support of the Government of Canada and the Nova Scotia Department of Tourism, Culture and Heritage.

As an organization operating in Cloverville, Nova Scotia, we acknowledge that the land on which we conduct our business is the traditional and unceded territory of the Mi'kmaq People. We pay our respects to the Elders, past and present, and express our gratitude for their stewardship of this land throughout the generations. We recognize Indigenous peoples' ongoing presence and contributions to our community and commit to fostering meaningful relationships based on mutual respect, understanding, and collaboration.

Contents

This book is dedicated to the two who planted
the first seeds of love in me,
my parents,
Alex and Minnie MacMaster.

The wild and rugged beauty of Cape Breton.

CHAPTER 1

Beginnings

"Nat! The phone's for you. It's a guy!"

It was 1991. I was nineteen and living on the fourth floor of a dormitory at the Nova Scotia Teachers College in Truro, about two hours from where I grew up. Halfway down the hall was a pay phone, shared among sixty girls, from which my friend shouted her message. Moments later, I was sitting down on a little chair, so curious, as she passed me the phone.

"Hello?"

"Hello, Natalie. My name is Donnell Leahy. You probably don't know me, but I'm a fiddler from Ontario."

"I DO know you! I have your cassette tape at home!"

Three years before this call, my cousin Danny had dropped by my family home in Cape Breton with a cassette of Donnell Leahy's music. Danny was a friend of the Leahys out in Ontario. He told me, "Nat, you need to hear this fiddler, incredible fiddler… and what a nice fella!"

Dad and I eagerly listened to that cassette in our living room, and I will tell you that I had never heard such fiddling before. Donnell's tone, precision, clarity, strength, and acrobatics left an unforgettable impression on my father and on me.

"Well, I'm in town tonight," Donnell continued, "and I was wondering if I could take you out to dinner."

"Sure," I replied, as my heart pounded with the thrill of it all.

"Could you bring along your fiddle, so I'll know who you are?"

Donnell had been playing shows with his siblings in Germany for six months, and there he had heard *4 on the Floor*, my debut recording, off a pirated cassette that his sister Denise had brought along. The copy had no cover or liner notes, yet she somehow knew that I was in my late teens and from Cape Breton, their mother Julie's homeland. When Donnell returned from Germany, he promptly headed out East with that cassette and my name in mind.

After twenty hours on the road, he arrived in Cape Breton and asked around about this fiddle player, Natalie MacMaster. He eventually met Allan Dewar, who happened to be a friend of mine and a fellow musician. Allan told Donnell that I was attending the Nova Scotia Teachers College and living in a dorm there. Donnell managed to find the number for my building in a phone book.

I was flattered that he'd asked me out, and I must have changed outfits three times before finally settling on a favourite lacy white blouse with pleated black dress pants and a classic black jean jacket. I strapped on my backpack fiddle case and went down to the lobby of Davis Hall.

It was all so exciting — like a blind date. Donnell had no idea what I looked like, and I had only that two-inch picture of him from the cover of his cassette. I arrived at the bottom of the stairs and there he was, clean and crisp with jet-black hair, tight curls, and large hazel eyes. My attention was quickly drawn to his hands, distinctly square in shape, strong yet graceful. Perhaps it was the musician in me to notice such a detail so early.

You know, it's funny, but I didn't bat an eye about meeting this "stranger" and driving away with him. Perhaps it was just a different era, but I also knew a bit about his family background which guided my instincts.

At the age of twelve, my parents took me to a special concert at the Inverness Arena in Cape Breton. We went to hear The Leahy Family, a talented group from Ontario whose eleven siblings fiddled, danced, sang, and played other instruments as well. There were so many of them, and all so multi-talented!

"See the mother there?" whispered my mom. "I used to step dance with her at concerts when we were young."

"Such a lovely lady," she continued.

"She must be lovely," I thought to myself, "look at her family."

Donnell was a gentleman on our date. He opened the car door for me, pulled out my chair at the table, and spoke to me with warmth. Even in the early 1990s, that behaviour was pretty rare in my circles and felt like something from days gone by. Donnell's outward displays of thoughtfulness were so sweet to me. I could see his good intentions and felt very safe with him.

We dined at The Glengarry, a local restaurant which seemed quite fancy at the time. While I don't remember much about dinner, my memories of our time afterwards are vivid.

"I have access to the music room on campus. Do you want to go play some tunes?" I was quite shy making the suggestion but felt I had to come up with something to extend the date since he had driven so far. We were both a bit awkward.

The space was set up with lots of instruments including a drum kit, saxophone, upright bass, and plenty of ukuleles. I hopped on the piano while Donnell played the fiddle for a little bit, and then I joined him on the fiddle. The tunes were standard repertoire, but we enjoyed just sitting there, talking, and playing music together. That went on for about an hour, at which point Donnell walked me the few yards back to Davis Hall. Guests were not allowed in after hours, so we started saying our goodbyes on the front steps of my dorm. Just before we finished, Donnell asked, "Would you like to go out again tomorrow night?"

I was delighted he'd asked, but had to reply, "I'm flying to Toronto tomorrow night to play at a square dance at the Army Navy hall on Saturday."

So, the next day, Donnell drove the twenty hours back to Ontario to meet me at the dance. It was there we started dating.

I Have a Love Story

Almost twenty-three years of marriage and seven children later, might anyone today guess that we broke up for nearly a decade before reuniting?

But my love story began long before then. I entered into it on the day of my birth, June 13, 1972.

I'm Natalie MacMaster, a Cape Bretoner born and raised, daughter to Alex and Minnie, and little sister to Kevin and David. We were raised in Troy, Cape Breton, Nova Scotia, in the home where Mom and Dad still live. I grew up surrounded by family and music. We weren't rich, but we weren't struggling either, at least not from my perspective, and I generally believed that how I was raised was how everyone else was raised.

As a child, I didn't grasp the unique beauty of Cape Breton, although I knew it was beautiful because everyone told me so. "But isn't a tree a tree?" I thought. "Isn't the ocean the same everywhere? And how else are people supposed to act but nice? Why are all these newcomers laughing so hard at how we talk and say things?" I didn't get it. But when you're a kid, you're not supposed to get it.

The trees, that ocean, those people — all of it shaped who I am today without my ever knowing. I can still feel the ocean breeze and smell the salt air when I think about my childhood. I can see the pretty pink roses growing wild along the roads that curved softly with the shoreline. I can look over the blues of the boundless water and watch the red and orange beams of the descending sun pierce through endless purple clouds. The crimson rays made the water sparkle for miles and miles.

To me, Cape Breton Island is a reflection of the Creator, an extension of love. My life found its first roots amidst all this beauty, and that life was so very good that it led me to identify them — beauty and goodness — with each other.

If culture has a cadence, the Island's unifying heartbeat was surely music. When my mother rocked me to sleep, she often vocally mimicked fiddle tunes, a skill we call jigging. On one occasion, I started crying a little because Mom wasn't home to put me down for the night. Dad came in after a few minutes and said, "I'll rock you." I wasn't very confident he'd do a good job.

After some instruction and a good while with me wriggling in his arms, he couldn't get the positioning just right, so he put me in a new position. Well, I came to love it so much that when Mom rocked me the next time in her regular fashion, I stopped her to say, "No! The new way." I must have been three or four. Even now, I can close my eyes and feel the long stride of the rock and Mom's vibrations while she jigged a fiddle tune with me in her arms.

As a young girl in Cape Breton, taking trips down to the ocean was always wonderful. The rugged shoreline of Creignish Beach was only a couple kilometres down the road. People didn't go away on vacation as much in those days. We made our own fun. There were countless places to explore, and I was fascinated by the coarse sand, the varieties of shells and sparkling rocks, the trickling brooks and moss-covered stones, the little crabs and minnows, and the seaweed and jellyfish washed up on the shore. It was nature's playground, a biology classroom in the wild.

The spectacular sandy beaches of Port Hood were always packed with locals and tourists. We lived about thirty minutes away and usually made it out once or twice during beach season. These trips were unquestionably worth it to me, but my parents, like so many who live near the ocean, were not beach people. As an adult, neither am I. Funny how a person can change like that. I used to suntan by slathering up with baby oil and lying on my tinfoil blanket. While everyone else seemed to acquire a gorgeous bronze glow, I had to burn several times before getting even a bit of colour. But I persevered and kept up with the trends!

My childhood was simple. I enjoyed crafts, dolls, music, and clowning around with my friends. Mom taught me step dancing when I was five, and I began playing piano at about the same time. I liked doing activities with the Girl Guides and was a Highland dancer for years.

When I was eight years old, I was asked to do a Highland dance at a concert. I felt a bit nervous and remember making a big mistake during the performance. I even had to stop dancing for a moment, which was so embarrassing. But I started up again and made it through to the end of the dance, at which point I ran off stage, sobbing to my mother. Mom took me in her arms and whispered nice things, but added, "You just need to practice a little harder for the next time." That was so important for me to hear.

My brother David is four years older than me and was constantly doing crazy things to get me laughing. Kevin, who is a year older than David, also liked to pick, tickle, and play practical jokes. They sometimes had me laughing so hard that I thought I might split in two! To this day, one of the highest compliments I can pay anyone is to say that they make me laugh as hard as my brothers did.

David would strut around, using a wrapping paper roll as a sword, claiming to be the king of the kitchen. When I laughed at David my whole body went limp. Sometimes I lost the strength to stand and dropped to the floor. He just struck me as hysterical, although I'm not sure he was so riotously amusing to anyone else.

Occasionally, I was so sick of my brothers teasing and poking at me that I'd turn wild and chase after them. How they'd run! One time I chased after David with a guitar over my head! I never did find out what I'd do if I caught them. But I'll tell you, as much as I screamed for Mom to rescue me from their antics, I also savoured the attention.

I loved my brothers very much despite their constant provoking. We didn't share many common interests, but that was okay. I remember Kevin once took me to the office at the end of the hall where we sat down to talk for a minute. I think I had my first crush at the time. He said he was always looking out for me, that I could tell him anything, and that he loved me. He just needed me to know that. We weren't ones to say, "I love you," so this was quite a big deal. I'll never forget it.

I often wandered around our one-acre yard, singing songs and pretending I was a famous vocalist. We had a hidden passage behind our house that led to a neighbour's unused property. The path crossed a section of rock, perhaps the foundation of something from long ago, over which we had to navigate ever so carefully before weaving through a section of overgrown bush.

To me, it was just the most magical experience. The path led to a clearing in the woods with magnificent chestnut trees and one oddly shaped cherry tree which grew sideways, not up but out. I called it my airplane tree because I could crawl to the end of one long, sturdy limb about ten feet long but only three or four feet off the ground. Bouncing at the end of this branch, I imagined that was how a real airplane might feel.

The chestnut trees provided a hefty supply of ammunition. My brothers and I, and sometimes our neighbours too, flung chestnuts at each other, although I seemed to be the only one who ever got whacked. My aim back then was just as it is now… terrible! I didn't play an ounce of sports. But I never flinched.

My parents were always such good and hardworking folks. Dad was employed for thirty-four years at the local pulp and paper mill, Stora Forest Industries, and had a pretty gruesome back shift schedule where he worked from seven at night until seven in the morning. Mom would often whisper, "Shhh, your father is sleeping," before chasing us outside to play. Dad worked alternating day shifts and night shifts through the decades. He never complained, was always appreciative, and constantly had other projects on the go to improve our property. Whether it was adding on to the house, rearranging the gardens at the front and back, or renovating some part of the place, there was always a better way to have things.

Mom stayed home to raise us. She put her heart and soul into being the best mother and was always the first one up and the last to bed. She nurtured us in so many ways, and our cupboards were always stocked with her fresh baking. The house was, without fail, clean, tidy, and pretty. There was no one more committed or on top of it; she never stopped. I remember asking her from time to time, "Mom, can you sit down with me?"

She'd answer, "Well, if I do, I'll never get back up!"

Even to this day, it's impressive what she takes on. No doubt this is a reflection of her own mother who ran their farm while her husband was out fishing and whose five brothers claimed she was "tougher than the boys."

The charitable spirit I witnessed in my mom and dad exemplified their devout faith. While they weren't overly knowledgeable about its intricacies, they lived the heart of it, which was to be virtuous, to forgive, to stay close to the Lord through prayer and the sacraments, to enjoy life, and to sacrifice for others. They were often doing something for someone else.

At that time in Cape Breton, locals in need were taken care of by the community more than government agencies. I remember a few people who had been dealt a tough hand in life with addictions, disabilities, or other issues. Some of them didn't have a proper home or vehicle and so would hitchhike a lot. My parents often gave them a ride somewhere or offered them a meal. We almost always had one of them come to our house for Easter or Christmas dinner. As kids, it wasn't much fun for us, but we knew it was just a little sacrifice to bear and sensed it was right to share what we had. And that was the point. Our faith meant living joy and love, but it also meant making sacrifices and serving other people. I sensed I was doing something meaningful. Being Catholic was never a compartment in my life. It was intertwined with every part of me.

As a parent, I've come to believe that the greatest way to love your children is to love your spouse first. That is what I saw in my home. The devotion was discreet but always there. It wasn't that my parents held hands or made showy signs of love, and we weren't an overly huggy bunch, but they did things that were perhaps even more meaningful.

They looked warmly at each other, spoke kindly and listened to one another, and never raised their voices. I clearly saw how much they enjoyed one another's company. I'm sure they had their disagreements, but I never heard them. Mom and Dad laughed together a lot and added a lightness to our days. And there was that quick kiss shared at the door before Dad left for the night shift. I always turned my head.

Living in this harmony influenced me more than I could ever have realized at the time, but now I recognize how their actions taught me so much.

I know there must have been times when Mom felt tired or disinterested in cooking food, but she did it anyway and I don't remember ever hearing her complain. She made hot, delicious meals, and even how she served them, always in nice dishes, always at the table, required extra care. You never had to get anything yourself either — it was brought to you. She wanted to give good things to her family and tells me now that it made her so happy to witness my delight when she made a dish I loved.

Mom loved to bake sweets in particular. I remember homemade peppermint patties, tweed squares, peanut butter cups, chocolate-covered coconut balls, lemon meringue pies, and chocolate cake with boiled brown sugar icing. Savoury meals included homemade chicken fingers and fries, steak and potatoes, ham and scalloped potatoes, ground beef with gravy and coleslaw, and turkey dinners with the best dressing and cranberry sauce made with cranberries picked by Dad. Homemade bread of some sort was baked almost daily. She surely loved us by serving these tried-and-true family recipes over and over again.

Although I must add that it was my father and the three of us children who did the loving on the days when we had to eat her famously overcooked roasts. In my mom's words, "Oh, it's just a little bit brown!"

I have a large extended family, and we gathered together for many events over the years. It could be for an anniversary, wedding, funeral, birthday, Christmas, or any other special occasion. I enjoyed every bit of time with my many cousins, aunts, uncles, and other relatives.

One cousin, Mary Elizabeth, was often at those gatherings. We were just a couple of weeks apart in age and we had very similar personalities, interests, and senses of humour. She was my best friend and we laughed a lot. I don't know if we were that funny to anyone else, but we certainly found ourselves to be hysterical and so enjoyed being silly together. I even peed my pants from laughing so hard! Yes, unbelievably embarrassing. Laughter and humour were big parts of my childhood and the Cape Breton way.

Those family parties rank among my absolute favourite childhood memories. As soon as I entered through the door, I was immediately transported, hearing the fiddle tunes rippin', smelling the aroma of homemade meatballs and cheesy dips, and watching the cousins run past. I'd join in and get sweaty playing games before making my way up to a bedroom to hang with the girls. Soon we'd be back playing chase and going outside. It was awesome being with a bunch of kids with whom I shared a family bond, and there was always the novelty of playing with other people's toys and checking out cool hiding places.

Throughout it all, the music was swirling through the air. The adults would gather in the music room where the piano was, and in the next room there would be a big table loaded with food. I could eat as much of anything as I wanted without having to ask, and the choice was enormous. I knew everyone around me was in good spirits, and since I saw my relatives mostly in these circumstances, they always seemed to be perfectly cheerful people from my young perspective.

When I had tuckered myself out, I'd go into the music room for a while. I loved listening to the fiddlers and watching them play. As I got older, I found myself running around less and less and sitting in the music room more and more. People didn't move from their seats, not even to go to the bathroom, it seemed. They'd find their spot and sit for hours, immersed in the music. It was like we were all hypnotized.

We were attentive listeners. Even my aunts, who had vibrant personalities, focused more on the music than on the party. They mostly drank tea through the night. My older cousins usually stood at the back or in the hallway, beer in hand, listening from a distance while catching up on the latest. Those in the music room barely spoke while the fiddler was playing. No one clapped along either. That would have masked the subtleties in the fiddling, and they all wanted to hear every detail of every note of every tune.

But it wasn't quiet in there either. People bounced their feet in perfect time, and when the fiddler swung into a favourite tune, someone would inevitably burst out with a lively "YIP!" or a "YEEHOO!" This stirred the energy levels and the fiddler responded with an extra boost to the music. Then sure enough, someone would land on the dance floor, steppin' 'er off, unable to help themselves. The dancing, the fiddling, the piano rhythms, and the tapping feet created one sound that swallowed us up.

Parties weren't limited to family gatherings. Many friends, neighbours, and musicians hosted house parties too. I enjoyed going to them just as much but in a different way. My cousins weren't there to run around with, so those nights were more calm and focused mostly on the music.

Unlike today, when recording music at an event is often prohibited, those with tape recorders would capture the magic of the night. Even the chit-chat between tunes, as well as all the jokes and laughter and noise, was fully present on those home cassettes. There were often multiple tapes of the same fiddler at the same party. Many good Cape Breton fiddlers did not have commercial recordings back then. Aside from being at a party, square dance, or similar event, getting a homemade cassette was the only way to hear many of those fiddlers play.

That's how I listened to a ton of music. It was really exciting to get a new recording, and everybody knew my mom adored them. People would often stop by to give her a copy of one they'd just made. It was like gold to us. Mom always had a cassette tape playing in the background, whether at home or in the car. The constant stream of fiddle music from those recordings ingrained in me an intimate knowledge of the Cape Breton style. Being surrounded by all this music in such a joyful environment, I couldn't help but love it.

Mom's Homemade Turkey Stuffing

Total time: 45 minutes *Serves:* 8

This dressing goes well with turkey or ham. If you're having a large crowd for dinner, you can double this recipe. It also freezes well in a Ziploc bag.

INGREDIENTS

- 7 medium-sized potatoes
- 7 tea biscuits (preferably 2 days old)
- ¾ cup butter plus 1 tbsp butter
- 1 small onion, finely diced
- 1 tbsp onion powder
- 3 tsp poultry seasoning
- 2 tsp dried sage
- 1 tsp salt
- ½ tsp pepper
- 2 tsp Mrs. Dash Original Blend Seasoning

METHOD

1. Peel, wash, chop, and boil the potatoes in a large pot.
2. While waiting for the potatoes to become tender, crumble the tea biscuits by hand or food processor until medium fine and set aside in a bowl.
3. Melt 1 tablespoon of butter in a frying pan then add
4. the diced onion, sautéing until soft and translucent.
5. Add onion powder, poultry seasoning, sage, salt, pepper, and Mrs. Dash to the cooked onion, mixing until combined. Turn off heat and add ¾ cup of butter to melt.
6. When the boiling potatoes become tender, drain water and mash.
7. Add the crumbled biscuits to the mashed potatoes.
8. Add the spice mixture to the potatoes and biscuits, mixing all together until well incorporated. Dressing should be moist. You may need to add a little extra melted butter if too dry.

Mom's Ground Beef with Gravy

Total time: 45 minutes *Serves: 4*

INGREDIENTS

1 small onion, finely chopped
1 tsp olive oil
1 pound ground beef
½ tsp salt
½ tsp pepper
1 tbsp onion powder
2 tsp Mrs. Dash Original Blend Seasoning
3 tbsp flour
2-3 cups water
2-3 tbsp Knorr concentrated liquid bouillon

METHOD

1. In a large frying pan, cook the onion in olive oil over medium heat, stirring often, until soft and lightly browned.
2. Add the ground beef and continue to fry until meat is cooked throughout and no longer pink. If necessary, drain any excess fat.
3. Add the salt, pepper, onion powder, and Mrs. Dash to the mixture, incorporating well.
4. Sprinkle the flour over the ground beef and mix throughout.
5. Slowly add 2 cups of water, stirring until thickened. Add in the bouillon and continue to mix.
6. Bring to a gentle boil and continue cooking for 2 minutes.
7. Turn off the heat, cover the pan, and let the beef and gravy rest to develop the flavour, about 10 minutes. If you find the gravy is too thick, add up to a cup of water until the desired consistency is achieved.
8. Serve the ground beef and gravy on top of mashed potatoes.

Tweed Squares

Total time: 2 hours *Makes: 24 squares*

CAKE BASE

INGREDIENTS

- 1½ cups flour
- 2 tsp baking powder
- ½ tsp salt
- ½ cup butter
- ½ cup sugar
- 2 egg yolks, reserving the whites
- ½ cup milk
- 1-ounce square (28 grams) semi-sweet chocolate, finely grated

METHOD

1. Grease and flour a 9x13 inch baking pan well or line with parchment paper. Preheat oven to 325°F (160°C).
2. In a large bowl, sift together the flour, baking powder, and salt.
3. In a separate bowl, beat together the butter and sugar until smooth. Then, add the egg yolks and beat until creamy.
4. Fold in the flour mixture, alternating with the milk, beginning and ending with the dry ingredients. Do not overmix.
5. In another bowl, beat the egg whites until soft peaks form and fold them into the cake batter.
6. Add in the grated chocolate, gently incorporating throughout.
7. Pour batter into the prepared pan and bake for 20–22 minutes or until a toothpick inserted in the centre comes out clean. Do not overbake the cake.
8. Cool on a wire rack. While the cake is cooling, make the buttercream frosting.

BUTTERCREAM FROSTING

INGREDIENTS

- ⅓ cup butter, room temperature
- 1½ cups powdered sugar
- 1 tsp vanilla extract
- 1 tbsp milk

METHOD

1. Cream together the butter, powdered sugar, and vanilla.
2. Add the milk to make a thick but spreadable frosting.
3. Spread the frosting on the cake base and let chill for 30 minutes.

CHOCOLATE TOPPING

INGREDIENTS

- 1 cup semi-sweet chocolate chips
- 2 tbsp butter

METHOD

1. Melt the chocolate and butter together in a microwave or in a double boiler.
2. Cool to lukewarm and spread quickly over the chilled frosting.
3. Let the chocolate set before cutting and serving, about 1 hour.

Aunt Mary Janet MacDonald's Porridge Brown Bread

Total time: *4 hours and 30 minutes* ***Serves:*** *3 loaves*

INGREDIENTS

3 cups water
2 tsp salt
1½ cups rolled oats
1 cup lukewarm water
1½ tsp white sugar
1½ tbsp active dry yeast
½ cup brown sugar
½ cup molasses
¾ cup vegetable oil
7 cups all-purpose flour

METHOD

1. Bring water and 1 teaspoon of salt to a boil and add oats. Simmer for 5 minutes.
2. Pour oat mixture into a large glass bowl and cool to lukewarm, about 45 minutes. Cover with a tea towel so that no skin forms on the porridge.
3. In a small bowl, add the lukewarm water, white sugar, and dry yeast, stirring gently to incorporate and dissolve the sugar.
4. Place the yeast mixture in a warm spot for 10 minutes.
5. Add the brown sugar, molasses, vegetable oil, and the other teaspoon of salt to the oat mixture after cooling. Mix well then add the yeast mixture.
6. Transfer the combined mixture to another large bowl and add 5 cups of all-purpose flour, 1 cup at a time to incorporate well.
7. Pour the last 2 cups of flour on a clean counter and place the dough on the floured surface, kneading in all the flour until blended well.
8. Take yet another large bowl and grease it with oil, then place the dough inside. Cover the top with plastic wrap and set aside for 1 hour and 30 minutes. Punch down.
9. Divide into 3 even pieces. Shape each one into a loaf and place in a standard size loaf pan. Let the bread rise for 1 hour in the pans.
10. Bake in the oven at 325°F (160°C) for 45 minutes.
11. Remove from the oven and brush the bread with butter if desired. This makes for a softer crust. If you like a harder crust, skip this step.

A little father-daughter moment as Dad bottlefeeds me.

Mom, Dad, Kevin, David, and me in our driveway.

My first Highland dancing kilt made from the Green Dress Gillies tartan.

(ABOVE) A little glimpse of my silly big brothers in action. Don't let my apparent disinterest fool you.

(LEFT) Creignish Beach will always be special to me.

Playing some tunes in the kitchen with Dad, my first fiddle teacher.

Getting to play with the best: Uncle Buddy on fiddle and John Morris Rankin on piano.

CHAPTER 2

Becoming a Musician

On January 6, 1972, the Canadian Broadcasting Corporation (CBC) aired a documentary called *Vanishing Cape Breton Fiddler*. It claimed that Cape Breton's fiddle culture was in danger of dying out because there were not enough young people carrying on the tradition.

Perhaps that was the catalyst needed to spawn a revival. A few activists led by Frank MacInnis formed the Cape Breton Fiddlers' Association soon after. They received permission from Father John Angus Rankin to host a three-day cultural event in July 1973 at St. Mary of the Angels parish in Glendale, Cape Breton, attracting over 130 fiddlers and more than 7,000 music enthusiasts. This pivotal moment ignited a renewed commitment to preserve our music traditions, and by the time I was a young girl, interest in cultural events was on an upward trend.

When I was nine and a half, I was gifted my first fiddle. My grand uncle, Charlie MacMaster, sent it up from Boston. He actually sent four fiddles in total to Mary Elizabeth's father, my Uncle Buddy MacMaster, with instructions to make sure they were given to any of the MacMasters who wanted them. Buddy called to see if anyone at our place was interested, and he mentioned on the phone that one of them was a three-quarter size. Smaller fiddles weren't as common back then, and I knew right away I would like that little fiddle. Dad and I drove the twenty minutes to Buddy's to get it. Dad taught me "Twinkle, Twinkle, Little

Star" that night, and I was so proud to have my very own instrument which fit me perfectly.

Over the next six months, I learned dozens of tunes with Dad's help and direction. Although I had never tried the full-sized fiddles in our house, I had been playing tunes on our piano, singing Gaelic songs, step dancing, and Highland dancing. Melodies were constantly in my head and I could hum a lot of tunes. If you can hum something you can learn it twice as easily on an instrument. Given my genes and the abundance of fiddle music that surrounded me since birth, by the time I picked up the fiddle, it was almost as if I had nine years of experience.

Even the subtle characteristics that make up the Cape Breton sound had become part of how I heard the melodies. I compare it to dialects in language. Think of one child growing up in England and another in Ireland. Although they both speak English, their accents are so very different. No one teaches them their accent. They just pick it up.

Around that time, my brother and I used Mom's tape recorder to make cassettes of ourselves singing silly songs and telling stories. I can remember a mock interview we did just days after I started fiddling.

David asked, "Where will you be performing next?"

"Oh, I'm flying to Calgary tomorrow to play with the symphony," I responded. "I'm going to be a star like my Uncle Buddy. Well, half of a star. I'll be half of a star."

I can tell you that from the first day I played the fiddle, I knew it was something I'd do forever.

Dad started me out with my first lessons, and even though he only scratched a bit on the fiddle, I learned quite a few tunes from him fairly naturally. Dad always had an incredible ear for the intricacies of the Cape Breton style.

My grandparents were big music enthusiasts according to my folks. Although my grandfathers, John Duncan MacMaster and John Beaton, had passed away before I made memories, I do recall my paternal grandmother, Sadie, with her distinctly hearty laugh and warm personality. Her body took on a subtle sway to the rhythm of the fiddle tunes while her feet tapped in perfect time as she sat energetically in her rocking chair. She lived with us for a short while and was clearly full of music.

It was my maternal grandmother whom I got to know very well. I was twenty-three when she passed. Maggie Ann Beaton loved fiddle music. When we'd go for a visit, I'd always play her some tunes and she would jig along to the melodies or sing them in Gaelic. "Everything is better in Gaelic," she'd declare, "because there just aren't enough words in English!"

Gramma was a well-known jigger of the tunes, and it was through this that she taught all her children to dance. When I'd get that fiddle out to play for Gramma, she'd close her eyes and tilt her head downward to focus, her whole body pulsing with every beat. Sometimes she'd even start dancing, hanging onto the back of a chair to take the pressure off her knees. I have never witnessed anyone more filled with the music. She would profess to me, "There's nothing as close to Heaven on God's green Earth as Scotch music. I think God must be playing it up there all the time!"

Uncle Buddy was my greatest musical influence. Although I never took lessons from him, I listened to and dissected his music more than that of any other fiddler. Many's the time I rewound the cassettes to hear his technique and beautiful repertoire as I worked to learn elements of his style.

I grew up watching Buddy play at many venues in Cape Breton including square dance halls, churches, community concert stages, living rooms, and our kitchen. He always looked spiffy and most often sported a white-collared shirt with a tie, dress pants, belt, shined shoes, perfectly combed hair set off to the side, and a cleanly shaven face. Even in my young years, I could see how loved and revered he was by all, and when he played, everyone listened. He was such a lively, spirited fiddler with a deep sweetness and undeniable lilt. We called him the king of the jigs. Buddy could raise the dead to dance.

According to my dad, Buddy was feistier in his youth, but I only knew him in his older years as a soft-spoken gentleman with a great sense of humour. Buddy played all around Cape Breton, throughout the rest of Canada and the United States, as well as overseas, and he never went halfway on a performance.

I can remember watching Buddy play at the square dances in Glencoe Mills, a community in the heart of Inverness County that has been hosting dances for decades. He'd have his sleeves rolled up and there would be two pools of sweat on either side of his chair where the drips collected after falling from his elbows. His body was so fully engaged that sometimes his chair moved with every beat. Buddy certainly left a permanent mark on our Cape Breton fiddling community.

But as great a fiddler as Buddy was, he was an even greater human being. He believed his purpose was to serve others. Rarely was a performance turned down, no matter how humble the circumstances or how difficult to accommodate. Sometimes he'd squeeze in a ribbon-cutting ceremony, a four-hour tavern session, and a full square dance, all in different communities, in a single day. He was a holy man who radiated goodness and charity, and I was always so proud to call him my uncle.

My first concert happened in the fall of 1982. I was ten years old and had been invited to play at the Glendale Hall on the west side of Cape Breton. I prepared two marches for the event, "The Glencoe March" and "Space Available." There were about a hundred people there, and when I got up to play, I scootched to the front of the chair so my feet would touch the floor.

Despite my anticipation I wasn't nervous, and I got through my tunes without a mistake. Mom and Dad told me they were pleased, but I already knew that. It was written all over their faces.

Soon after that performance, Dad remarked, "I think it's time to put you in lessons." Mom had heard about Stan Chapman, a renowned and wonderful fiddle teacher, who lived forty-five minutes away in Antigonish. She enrolled me and I was excited to start with him.

Stan was caring, gentle, and always very encouraging. All of the music I'd learned up to that point had been by ear, and while Stan continued to teach me in this way, he also introduced me to the basics of how to read notes. I wasn't very keen on that, but Stan offered just the right balance of both that kept me eager to keep on with the lessons.

Stan provided a solid foundation in the fundamentals of Cape Breton fiddling and expanded my repertoire tremendously. I particularly remember learning the "cuts," a very specific fiddling technique that involves a triplet of bow movements, done quickly, to simulate a rippling effect within a tune. I thought cuts were the coolest and I was eager to learn them. Stan taught me what to do and then I went home to develop the skill. I went through the cuts slowly, patiently, and then a little quicker and quicker, until I was eventually able to make them sound pretty good. That was the first time I practiced for a whole hour. I remember proudly showing off my new cuts to Dad as he sat in the kitchen on the rocking chair.

By the time I was thirteen, I was playing quite a variety of events throughout the Island. Performing was always a big deal to me. I didn't care about anything as much as I cared about how well I played the fiddle; even casual performances gave me butterflies. I preferred listening to playing, probably because I was never nearly as good as I wanted to be. If I didn't play my best, it would ruin my night. But only I knew that.

All the communities like Judique, Port Hood, Mabou, Inverness, Broadcove, Margaree, and Cheticamp, up through the highlands, over Baddeck and Sydney way, as well as other regions, hosted special events through the summer to celebrate community and culture. Each relied on the talent in the area for entertainment. Our local publication, *The Inverness Oran*, provided a great source of advertisement for these events, and my mother cut and saved many clippings.

I'm sure it was a benefit to be the niece of Buddy MacMaster as well as the daughter of Minnie Beaton, who had been a popular step dancer in her day. In fact, Dad often joked that he never had his own identity. He would say, "Growing up I was always Buddy MacMaster's brother. And then I married your mom and became Minnie Beaton's husband. And then you started fiddling and I became Natalie MacMaster's father!"

I also had many other popular musical relatives: my Aunt Betty Lou Beaton played the piano, my Aunt Genevieve Whalen was a vocalist and TV show personality, and my third cousin, John Allan Cameron, enjoyed many years of fame and popularity.

It was mostly men who played fiddle at that time, but there were a few female players as well, like Theresa MacLellan, Winnie Chafe, Anne MacDonald, and Mary MacDonald. I did not process or analyze this fact in any way. It just was what it was. When I began fiddling, a few other girls started roughly around the same time including Jackie Dunn, Stephanie Wills, Wendy MacIsaac, and Tara Lynne Touesnard. We were a minority then, so being a young female fiddler was a bit of a novelty.

There was a healthy number of younger guys playing at that time as well, like Ashley MacIsaac, Rodney MacDonald, Glenn Graham, Neil Beaton, and Dwayne Côté. Through playing music together over the years we all became friends. A group of us played with each other so often that they started calling us "The Special Seven." Many hours were spent with some of them at the practice sessions sponsored by the Cape Breton Fiddlers' Association, and we found fun in the comradery while learning from one another.

I was steeped in a lively music culture that greatly contributed to my development as a musician. Thank God for all those communities that offered so many outlets to all levels of players, amateurs and professionals alike. I always said yes to the invitations, and Mom and Dad carted me around to every nook and cranny of the Island, no matter how small or far away.

I've heard it said that playing in front of an audience is like practicing twice. It's so true. Beyond playing the fiddle, I was also developing and organizing a repertoire, playing with various accompaniment, and navigating through changing environments and audiences. I was learning how to conduct myself and, without knowing it, honing my craft on stage.

Timing is an important element of Cape Breton fiddling, and the music should feel energetic without feeling rushed. Mom and Dad both knew it when they heard it and were a good gauge of how well I played at a performance. They always offered some healthy critique on the drive home. It wasn't always positive. Sometimes they'd say, "You were a little rushed and losing the feel." Or, if it was really fast, Dad would say, "You were goin' like a bat outta hell!" That was never a good thing. Criticism is easier to take when you're young, and as such, is the best time to master the art of its receipt.

No matter what they told me, it was always the truth and they gave it to me straight. Dad just had to give the right wink or nod of the head, even from across the hall, and that was all the assurance I needed. Sometimes Mom told me, "It was so friggin' good," and on a rare occasion I'd even hear Dad say, "You're a dandy, Nat." The sweetness with which he delivered this endearing term assured me of his love and pride.

During the drive home, snuggled under the blanket Mom always threw in the back seat, I felt a great sense of peace and contentment knowing I had tried my best, earned a few dollars, made my parents proud, and brought happiness to a few people.

A treasured experience in my early days was getting invited to the World's Fair, Expo 86, in Vancouver, British Columbia. I was fourteen when I received a call from John Shaw, a Gaelic researcher and singer from our community who had been asked to organize a group of performers to represent the music culture of Cape Breton Island. I squealed when I got off the phone. Mom and Dad were thrilled, and we immediately made plans for the three of us to go. This marked my first time on an airplane, and I flew from one ocean right across the country to another.

I managed to convince my folks to also bring along Mary Elizabeth. At our hotel in Vancouver, the pair of us hung out the window, shouting to passersby like two old drunken ladies, with pop bottles disguised in brown paper bags and our teeth hidden under curled lips as if we were toothless! Cape Breton humour at its finest?

Spanning over seventy hectares along False Creek in the heart of Vancouver, the exposition attracted twenty-two million visitors, including Prince Charles and Princess Diana. It featured pavilions from fifty-four nations as well as plazas, theatres, exhibits, restaurants, and rides, which we loved to frequent during our free time.

The entertainment world was represented by a variety of global performers, including dance troupes, comedians, school bands, and pop and country stars. About fifteen fiddlers, Gaelic singers, piano players, guitarists, and step dancers from Cape Breton went over to perform three concerts a day for two weeks. I did a solo at every show, performed fiddle duets with my friend Jackie Dunn, played for some dancers, and joined in all the grand finales. Although I was naturally quite shy, I enjoyed the challenge of growth, the adventure of travel, and the opportunity to do something special. Expo 86 was an important stepping stone.

Not only did my mom and dad accompany me on that trip, they accommodated me with everything in every way and not once did I sense it was drudgery for them. They did the same for my brothers as well. Kevin and David were into sports, and we'd all head off for a hockey tournament on a weekend. Mom brought a big victory bell she'd shake like crazy for the goals and I followed her example, cheering on my brothers from the stands. My parents were so supportive and encouraging of all our activities.

At the time, I thought this was just what parents did. Now I can see how deeply they loved us and the inner grace they must have possessed to remain lighthearted and positive. They focused less on their needs and more on ours. Yet, with all this catering, they never sacrificed a loving authority. Mom had a good bit of spice in her when it was needed, and she worked her magic to keep us in line. We were far from perfect, especially as teenagers with typical curiosities that occasionally compelled us to push boundaries.

If we stepped out of line and Dad heard about it, there'd be consequences. Fortunately, our mischief was mostly mild and so was Dad's discipline. But we knew a lion lived under his unassuming exterior, ready to be unleashed if necessary. More than that, we just respected him so much that none of us ever incurred his full wrath. Despite having developed some good habits, it takes time to value virtue, to desire it, and then to mould the will. Sometimes a lifetime.

When I was fifteen, I received an invitation to play at the 1987 Vancouver Folk Music Festival. My name and reputation had started to develop, which led to more travel throughout Canada and the United States at various Celtic and folk music festivals and events. Another fifteen-year-old fiddler was featured at the festival as well, and I gravitated towards her because we were both fiddling girls the same age. Her name was Alison Krauss. She came from a very authentic culture of bluegrass music and was likable, pretty, talented, and seemed a bit shy like myself. And she could play that fiddle, no doubt! She left a lasting impression on me.

Through these festivals, my mind was opened to new and worldly ways of fiddling. There were so many different styles from bluegrass and jazz to Cajun and Irish, Texas swing, Shetland, Norwegian, Mexican, and many more. Each had an individual character which unveiled the unique nuances of my own.

For instance, curious minds would sometimes ask me, "How do you tap your foot to the music? Where does that come from?"

It forced me to think, "Yeah, where does that come from?" Honestly, I really didn't know.

Foot pounding is very much a part of the Cape Breton fiddle culture, but when I learned to play, no one taught me how to tap my foot. When I watched other fiddlers, it didn't register that they were tapping their feet. As a result, when I began playing, I just tapped without ever noticing.

Although I was immersed in the fiddle culture of Cape Breton, other types of music were also enjoyable. "Saturday Night" by the Bay City Rollers, "Rhinestone Cowboy" by Glen Campbell, and "Voulez-Vous" by ABBA got lots of spins on our record player. These melodies were often running through my head along with bits of fiddle tunes. I just had a great fondness for any music.

One night back in Cape Breton when I was sixteen, I was sitting in the kitchen rocking chair after supper as we listened to *Scottish Strings*, a local Celtic music radio program. That's when I heard Paul MacDonald, a fiddler my age from Prince Edward Island. We had played with each other a couple times before, and the station was playing a track from his new cassette tape. This took me by surprise, and I recall thinking, "He's got a recording out?"

I couldn't comprehend a teenager thinking they were good enough to make a record. The thought didn't come to me in a critical way, I just couldn't have imagined feeling that confident at sixteen. It had never crossed my mind that someone could be good enough to make a record before they were well into adulthood; even Buddy MacMaster hadn't made a studio recording until he was sixty-four.

Still, Paul *had* made a record. I was captivated by this and listened intently as the track went on. It was excellent, and he positively was more than good enough. By the end, I distinctly remember thinking, "If he can do it, so can I."

Over the next few days, I pondered the concept of recording but kept the idea to myself. The only thing holding me back was the fear of looking boastful. Who was I to think I was good enough to record music at sixteen years old? But deep down, I knew I had it in me. I soon chose to focus on the excitement of this concept rather than on my fears about how I might be perceived. When I finally shared these thoughts with my parents, they were calmly positive about the idea and didn't seem to doubt it for a second.

To this day, material is still my greatest concern musically. I eventually settled on eight tracks which I picked from old cassette tapes of my favourite fiddlers including Buddy MacMaster, Arthur Muise, Kinnon Beaton, Donald Angus Beaton, Winston

"Scotty" Fitzgerald, Willie Kennedy, Angus and Cameron Chisholm, Jerry Holland, Howie MacDonald, John Morris Rankin, Dougie MacDonald, John Campbell, and Bill Lamey.

I learned so much from listening to those recordings. I was especially taken by one of Eileen Ivers and Séamus Egan that had been taped at The Turning Point in New York. Mom had gotten a copy of it from our American friends, Mike Denney and Marleen Podorowsky. I was captivated by this new and incredibly fancy sound, so much so that I included a medley of their tunes entitled "Blackberry Blossom" on my list of chosen material.

"Happy Go Lucky" was one of the more challenging tunes I was eager to record. Playing it meant I would have to shift my hand up on the fingerboard, a skill I had not yet tried. While I certainly didn't have great technique, I was motivated by the challenge and practiced the shift over and over until I got it. If I were to play "Happy Go Lucky" today, I don't think I'd get through it on the first try. The shift in the second part will always be tough for me.

After choosing the music, I picked my three favourite accompanists who I hoped would join me. There was Dave MacIsaac, undoubtedly one of the top guitarists for Cape Breton fiddle music, and my Aunt Betty Lou and John Morris Rankin, who I'd played with on many occasions and were two of the best piano players on the Island. But asking them to play on my record was another story.

"You have to go ask them yourself," Mom insisted. "It's your record, it's your project. I'm not asking them for you." I was so shy, even when approaching my own aunt. I did ask them, on the same night when all three were conveniently at one of Betty Lou's house parties. They graciously said yes, and I was completely confident I had the best musicians on the project.

Beyond asking accompanists, there were so many practical details to take care of which my mother embraced, diving in like she always did. With all the support from the people most important to me, I never gave my initial doubts a second thought. I prepared as best I could, and after about four months of planning we drove up to Solar Audio Recording Studio in Halifax, Nova Scotia.

This was my first time in a studio. I recall the smell of electronics, all the audio gear, the huge console and speakers, and the sleek black leather couch that sat at the back of the control room. There was a big grand piano out in the recording space, and soundproof dividers had been set up to create isolation between the musicians. I had to wear headphones while playing, which was a new experience and took a moment to get used to.

I was absolutely nervous, but I was right where I wanted to be. I loved the dynamic among us all. Dave was so very comical. He and John Morris were good friends who fed off one another all day. My Aunt Betty Lou was possibly the funniest of them all and was just such a cool lady. Between takes, I sat listening to them, the supposedly mature adults, and all their riotous banter. Through all the humour, they offered direction and encouragement and were very supportive. They'd tell me, "You're tough as nails, Nat!"

We recorded and even mixed that whole cassette in a day. During the three-hour drive back home, we listened to the copy of *4 on the Floor* they had given us. I couldn't wipe the smile off my face. Mom and Dad were thrilled and it felt like a dream. Knowing I had my own recording was beyond any preconceived feeling and I was just so happy. I don't recall experiencing that degree of satisfaction for any music accomplishment since. Even though I was ecstatic, I eventually fell asleep with my pillow and blanket in the back seat.

That summer, a boatload of those cassettes were sold out of the trunk of our car. We brought them along to the dozens of community events where I performed. Dad had the stash of tapes ready, and when someone inquired about them, the trunk would open up. This drew the attention of curious onlookers who began to form a queue behind the vehicle. Mom and I also went around to the local gift shops to stock their shelves with whatever orders they requested. Being one of only a few young fiddlers with a record did wonders for my confidence. It was a most magical time in my music world.

I started at the Nova Scotia Teachers College in 1990 at age eighteen. As I was moving into the campus dorm on the first day, some boisterous lady hollered out her window, "Natalie MacMaster is coming here!" That was Janice Aucoin, a fun and fiery French girl from Cheticamp, Cape Breton, and we became good buddies during my time at college. I have wonderful memories from my days there with her, Mindy, Gaye, and the many other great friends I made.

My greatest motivation for attending teachers college was to secure a career which would allow me to continue fiddling and performing. Music was my passion, but I also adored children and thought I could manage teaching with the travel I was doing during the summer season, weekends, and holidays. Those were busier times in the music industry, and with my steadily increasing number of performances and events, this plan seemed to make a lot of sense.

Later in my first year of college, I heard a beautiful voice coming from the speakers in Janice's room. I asked her, "Who is that you're listening to?"

"Alison Krauss."

"Wait, WHAT?" I exclaimed. "That can't be! She sings?"

"It must be the same Alison," I thought, "but didn't she only play the fiddle?" Janice flashed the cover and sure enough, it was Alison! What a uniquely beautiful voice. Janice was so excited that I had met and played with her.

A significant performing experience came along in the summer after my freshman year. *The Cape Breton Summertime Revue* was a popular touring entourage that highlighted the music and humour of the Island. My parents and the community considered *The Revue* the crème de la crème of Cape Breton shows, so I was very honoured to join the cast for the 1991 season.

I'm sure there are people who look at me now and see a confident performer. Well, I've had to become that. I gained confidence because I was thrust into so many sink-or-swim scenarios. Before that summer, I almost always used to sit in a chair to play and avoided speaking into a microphone. Even when there were occasions I could have used the mic, I ducked out and only spoke when necessary. Since I was usually part of group events, someone else almost always introduced me.

Well, surprise, surprise! The director of *The Revue* asked me to do all my playing standing up and even gave me a speaking role in one of the skits. I was so nervous that I had knots in my stomach for days. But I wasn't going to say no since I didn't want to be the person who couldn't do it. I trusted the director's expertise and adapted to the needs of the production. The challenge of stepping out of my comfort zone was a great opportunity to grow and improve.

After two weeks of intense daily rehearsals, we set out for a summer filled with shows. I was so proud to be a part of it all and very excited for my family to see me on opening night. While they enjoyed the whole show, the next day Mom told me what she really thought. "You looked lifeless on stage," she declared. "It seemed as if you were asleep up there! Do something. Move!"

Her words rendered me speechless, and I had none of my usual retorts. After letting the idea sink in, I knew she was right. A little smile didn't translate much with an audience forty feet away, and I did feel awkward just standing there.

The next time, I tried doing "something" to show some liveliness, but everything felt so forced and unnatural. I felt like an idiot, actually. I had no moves and certainly never witnessed any other fiddlers moving around while they played.

But I persisted. Over the course of days and weeks, I slowly got more comfortable playing while standing up. I let loose and allowed myself to feel the music more than think, to listen to my bandmates, to absorb what I heard around me, and to join with the energy of an audience. I don't know quite how it happened, but something changed in me. I developed the ability to outwardly convey my inward interpretation of the music. In fact, I must have conveyed it too forcefully because when my brother David saw me perform a while later, he said, "Natley! You look like a doink up there, jumpin' all over the place. What's that all about? Settle down!"

And so, with every new performance, I evolved, becoming increasingly aware of the precious connection I was making with a crowd. How could I best deliver what I felt inside? What were THEY receiving? Sometimes people hear with their eyes. I adopted a different perspective and came to understand my role as a conduit of music. It wasn't always easy, and there were things I had to learn to deal with.

Performing includes a complex balance of focuses: playing well, repertoire, arrangements, technical components, crowd dynamics, musical response, managing adrenaline, connecting with the band, set flow, verbal communication, spontaneity, and so much more. I imagine a lot of people watch a seasoned performer and assume it's just natural, but so much of it is learned. Attaining the mental freedom necessary to become a musical vessel while still holding in mind all the things you need to think about is a specific balance that's acquired through years of experience.

I was now doing some solo shows with my own band. People were spending their money to hear me play, and the pressure and excitement were rising. I remember being backstage before a show and getting quite nervous. My hands were trembling, so I tried warming up some more. As I ran through my piece, I could feel the shakiness under my bow. This caused more nervousness. I did not like this feeling, not one bit.

When I got to the stage, my performance was less than it should have been and the shaking ruined the musicality. It was all I could do to focus and just try to get through it.

This pattern continued over the next while, and I was getting sick and tired of it.

"Enough!" I finally thought, "I can't take this. Stop it. Stop being so nervous."

I tried stretches and warmups. I prayed. How would I get rid of this?

Eventually I tried to command my nerves. I recognized that the nerves and shakiness were an energy, and energy is good for a performance. So I worked to embrace it and transform those unavoidable nerves into strength and power to yield a mighty performance. It was a mind game, but after some time and working through lots of situations, I was able to master my nerves.

Even today I still feel that nervous energy before I go on every stage, but I've come to love the feeling. I embrace, command, and direct it to bring vitality to my performance. It's a reminder that I still care so deeply about the quality of my delivery. I've even come to see it as a gift from God.

People often say, "Be who you are." It sounds nice, but if I had stayed who I was in my youth, I might never have spoken into a microphone or developed as an entertainer. It's not who I am by nature, and it's certainly not who I was. I believe I'm still becoming who I am, who I want to be, and who I'm meant to be both as an artist and as a human being.

It was after a year at college that I received Donnell's phone call.

Right from the beginning, we had a lot of laughs. We even got stopped for speeding a number of times because we were laughing so hard. Once Donnell had me going, he didn't let up. He had a clever and slightly mischievous sense of humour.

I recall those years fondly: the airport pickups and drop-offs, the adventures on the road, and meeting his wonderful family for the first time. Oh, I was as nervous as I'd ever been for anything! At nineteen, I had a good bit of travel and stage experience, had learned the art of meeting people and navigating a crowd, and had been through numerous business negotiations. But this was just so different. Now my heart was in the game, and I really cared about the impression I was about to make. I had a boatload of respect for Donnell and I just sensed that he was a reflection of some wondrous, magical existence that was his home life.

When we arrived at their farmhouse on the top of a hill, my palms were sweaty and my heart was pounding. "This is it," I thought. "Calm down, girl!"

Donnell's mother, Julie, was delightfully calm and gracious. I felt our shared

Cape Breton spirit. Through her actions she reassured me that I was welcomed and understood. She put me at ease, and I couldn't help but think, "Here is my comfort zone."

Donnell's father though! Frank's gaze was striking as he extended his large, rough farm hand for a shake. I wasn't at all sure what he was thinking, but it seemed clear to me he was always thinking about something. His voice was pointed and confident in a respectful sort of way, and no conversation was ever surface talk. He was inquisitive, thoughtful, a bit mysterious, full of personality, and quite witty. Frank possessed more charm than anyone I'd ever encountered and I was in awe of his domain.

I met Donnell's ten siblings in fragments. Most of them weren't living at the homestead by that point and his oldest sister was married with a child. The ones who were home were thoroughly welcoming. Donnell's older sisters had such distinctly vibrant personalities that I could tell they were a party waiting to happen.

I'll never forget the time I offered to help with the dishes after a meal. The pile was mighty, and at that point I honestly don't think I had ever washed dishes before, except maybe in home economics class in ninth grade.

I went to the sink and proceeded to try and gently pile every last cup, fork, plate, dish, and pot into that sink, only to discover it couldn't be done. When Mom washed the dishes at home, I was sure she just put everything in the water all at once. Now what was I supposed to do?

I can't remember how I got out of that one, but I knew my inexperience must have been glaringly obvious to everyone. I'm sure I turned a few shades and it still embarrasses me today just thinking about it.

I had not a speck of experience with farming prior to my first visit to the Leahy home. So when Donnell decided it would be a nice day to take me for a walk in the field with the cows, I trusted it was a safe thing to do but remained close. He cautioned me to watch out for "that wild, white cow," which, of course, I saw almost immediately.

"Oh my gosh, Donnell, it's there!" I pointed, surprised yet proud I'd found it. Genuinely petrified, my body went stiff. "Donnell, help! I'm scared. What do we do?"

He responded with some sort of apathetic shrug.

"What?" I thought, annoyed by his apparent indifference. I fired back, "If you don't help me here, I'm not talking to you!"

"Alright," he said casually, walking away.

I pleaded for his help, at which point he returned and said, "I thought you weren't talking to me." Turns out, most of the cows in that field were white and none of them were wild!

Although ours was a long-distance relationship, I found it a healthy one because it was based less on physical presence and more on talk and trust. When we did fly in for a visit, it was all the more special and lasted a good number of days.

Donnell and I used to go out and do some country dancing. I had no clue what I was doing at the start but thought it was the coolest thing. I think Donnell must have known how proud I was to show him off on the dance floor because I just couldn't stop smiling while we were dancing. Still can't! He was such a good leader that I didn't have to do much to look the part, but it did take me a fair bit of time to learn the basics. We usually danced at a bar with either my friends or his, depending on which province we were in.

Donnell came and played at the Doryman Tavern in Cheticamp about a year into dating. I was so proud to watch him play before this crowd of fiddle fanatics. On stage, he had an unbelievable ability to command the attention of an audience through his instrument.

I recently came across a letter I wrote to Donnell from that time. In it, I reminded him that I loved him. Yes, we eventually came to say "I love you" in that first period of dating. It was exciting to hear and exciting to say, and we certainly meant it. But while my feelings of attraction and affection for Donnell were genuine, time revealed it was a young love and not the kind that compelled us to commit forever.

The popularity of our individual music was growing swiftly, and the world was beckoning to each of us with its many opportunities. Our complex schedules became progressively harder to wrangle, and we were still quite young to dive into a relationship for life. These distractions and our immaturity ultimately led us to part ways after almost two years of dating. I was twenty and Donnell was twenty-four.

(ABOVE) My paternal grandparents, John Duncan and Sadie MacMaster.

My maternal grandparents, John and Maggie Ann Beaton.

My first studio recording, *4 on the Floor.*

Gramma Sadie stops to listen.

Mom and I pause for a moment at Kaye White's house in Detroit before heading out to play at a square dance.

(ABOVE) My dear buddies from college: Mindy Gillis (centre), Janice Aucoin (right), and Gaye Mombourquette (not pictured).

(LEFT) Me with my cousin and best friend, Mary Elizabeth, on prom night.

A little tune time with my new boyfriend, Donnell Leahy.

Exciting times with the cast of *The Cape Breton Summertime Revue*: Neil Robertson, Berkley Lamey, Max MacDonald, Bette MacDonald, Maynard Morrison, me, Matt Minglewood, Doris Mason, and Fred Lavery.

John Morris Rankin, Betty Lou Beaton, and Dave MacIsaac pose for a quick photo during the creation of my first studio recording, *4 on the Floor*.

The whole Cape Breton entourage performing in the Folklife Pavilion at EXPO 86. From left to right: Donald MacLellan, Dave MacIsaac, John Morris Rankin, Alex Francis MacKay, John Shaw, Jackie Dunn, and me.

A typical flushed-face stare while "sawing" the last note of a performance.

CHAPTER 3

Broadening My Horizons

"Would you guys mind opening tonight's concert? It's for Carlos Santana."

I was playing at the Riverbend Festival in Chattanooga, Tennessee, when I received that request. It was a bright and beautiful day in June of 1995, and sprawls of people were happily meandering around the hilly grounds.

The band previously booked had to cancel at the last minute, so I said, "Yeah, sure!"

I barely knew Santana's name, but Dave MacIsaac was a huge fan. "Natalie, don't you know 'Black Magic Woman'?" he asked, incredulous that I knew so little about the beloved guitarist who had pioneered a fusion of rock and Latin jazz.

We were told we would be performing on a 200 foot-long barge floating just off the shore. The Coca-Cola Stage stood twenty-two feet above the lower deck and had to be accessed by numerous stairs.

By the time the concert was about to begin, an estimated 80,000 people were out there in front of the barge. We had a half-hour slot and I was over the moon about the opportunity to share our Cape Breton fiddle tunes in such a phenomenal setting. The great pianist Tracey Dares was with Dave and me to round out our trio. While we may not have had a ten-piece band joining us, we were authentic, and under the last-minute circumstances, I was committed, fully ignited, and confident in the skills and determination of my fellow musicians.

My aim was to transform this crowd, a feat which would rely on my choice of material, the flow of our set, our dynamics, and the quality of our delivery. It was up to us. This was part of the thrill of making music. If successful, we would unleash the energy of thousands of people grooving, clapping, and cheering in unison.

I felt like a horse behind the gate, jittery with adrenaline. The hardest part of any performance is often the wait just before you go on stage. Would they like me? Would they get my music? The Cape Breton style had never let me down and I placed my trust in that.

During our opening segment I was just driv'n 'er. Do you know that expression? To "drive 'er" means to give it your all. Tracey and Dave were pulsing out the rhythm like a freight train. We were so far away from the crowd, but I could see people swaying to the music. That was a good sign. Our first number garnered respectful applause, but I wanted more.

I had saved our most energetic piece for the end and was hopeful we could get them rockin'. It was a traditional medley that started with a march, moved into some strathspeys, which are intense Scottish tunes with spunky rhythms, and finished with a couple of reels. Now wouldn't you know, somewhere during the reels I broke my D string? Yup! Driv'n 'er so hard she snapped!

Desperation and experience kicked in. Dave instinctively picked out a melody on his guitar while I grooved on one string for a few moments before fiddling and step dancing simultaneously. Tracey professionally continued to pound it out and support this circus. I was bursting with determination, and if there had been a ring of fire on stage, I would have jumped through it!

Our ending moment was a wild jumble of notes, energy, dancing, and groove, which was effective enough to garner huge applause from this wonderfully receptive crowd. Carlos Santana was there too, watching from side stage.

When we got off, I blurted out to him, "I broke a string!"

He said, "You need to do what B.B. King does and take along a spare."

We all had a chuckle about that. And you know what, I've brought along a spare fiddle to every performance since then. Thanks for the tip, Carlos!

What a thrill to be hangin' with him for a few moments before he headed on stage to play for his legions of fans. Good times.

The growth I experienced during the mid-'90s was wonderfully fulfilling and even addictive. I eventually went from playing with piano accompaniment as a duo to having a guitarist join us in a trio setting, then on to a four-piece with percussion, a five-piece with bass, and finally a six-piece after adding a piper. It was like a musician's playground, discovering how to tastefully incorporate all these colourful new sounds. I loved the creativity and wanted to be a powerhouse on stage to more accurately represent the sound and spirit I heard in my head. I explored the theatrics of dancing while this dynamic band rocked out. The music became more impactful that way, especially for those who did not understand fiddling.

The pop culture of my youth affected how I heard things. The dynamic beats of Michael Jackson, the vocal prowess of Whitney Houston, and the electrifying synth-pop of Duran Duran no doubt influenced my sensibilities. The gentler songs of Anne Murray, Melissa Manchester, and ABBA that I enjoyed were quite the contrast to my older brothers' favourite recordings by Ozzy Osbourne, Led Zeppelin, Pink Floyd, Def Leppard, and AC/DC, which also started to grow on me.

By this point, I had learned ninety percent of my repertoire by ear. I picked up new tunes from musicians in other countries during my travels, like the time I was teaching at Sabhal Mòr Ostaig, a traditional music school in the Isle of Skye, Scotland. After completing my daily lessons, I gathered with the other instructors for a jam session, and it was there I heard "Catharsis," just a ripper of a G minor reel. I had never heard such a cool tune.

Luckily for me, the nature of those jam sessions meant we played tunes multiple times, which gave me a chance to memorize the music and then bring it back home. I recorded "Catharsis" on *No Boundaries*, and it ended up being the most popular track. Warner Music Canada even chose it as the first release and funded an accompanying video.

I later found out Amy Cann was the composer. Thanks, Amy. You know, I hear that tune everywhere now. Amazing how tunes travel.

Having the right material was paramount, and I spent hours and hours researching. One day, after failing in a search to find something that was gritty, energetic, and in a minor key, I thought, "Where am I going to find a tune like this? Surely there's a fiery minor piece somewhere, maybe a jig or a reel. But I've gone through so many books already. It's just not here!"

I had the concept in mind but no melody to play. That's when it dawned on me. "I'll have to write one."

I had written tunes before but with little motivation. Considering the endless melodies in the old tune books, a variety of compact discs at my fingertips, and cassette tapes containing thousands of untapped gems, I saw no reason to invest my energy in writing something. I assumed I just didn't have the gift.

That way of thinking changed in an instant. I tried again with renewed purpose, working to create a tune that would satisfy my vision. That's the day I became a composer. "David's Jig" was the answer I was looking for.

David's Jig

Natalie MacMaster

My life was swirling with calls and requests, trips and experiences, and events and people. Things accelerated to the point where I played hundreds of shows throughout my college years. I acquired management and multiple booking agents, and by my third year of college I had accumulated numerous awards and only attended school part time.

I was often thrust into new situations and pulled out of my comfort zone. One time, I received a phone call from a fellow in Prince Edward Island who asked if I'd be willing to do an advertisement for Farmers Milk. I said, "Sure!" with no thought of negotiations or details or expectations. I just figured it would be cool to be in a commercial.

What I didn't realize was the extent of the campaign. For weeks, my face was on every milk carton across the Maritime provinces, and a huge billboard, with images of me dancing, fiddling, and swirling, towered near the Macdonald Bridge in Halifax. That opportunity turned out to be an incredibly valuable marketing tool and raised my profile considerably in our locale.

I went on to do a couple of regional car commercials for Pontiac and Subaru. Then came the big national ad campaign for Tim Hortons. Woo wee! That was an elaborate shoot which included my band, the tour bus, and multiple performance venues. The exposure gave me a huge boost in the marketplace. I befriended Ron Joyce, the owner of the company back then, and played at a number of functions both for him and for Tim Hortons. If travel arrangements got tricky, he would just pick me up in his private jet. God rest his soul.

I got to connect with a lot of legendary musicians in the industry as well. Whether it was Angus Young with AC/DC at a Warner Music Canada party, or Diana Krall and Art Garfunkel on a luxury ocean liner to Antarctica for the millennium, it was a heady time, hobnobbing with the who's who. These interactions helped me gain a better understanding of myself, and I came to learn how much I loved people, conversation, gourmet food, and red wine!

I especially valued the unique bond of musicians which transcended any differences. The unity amongst us was something I came to treasure. Even though our lifestyles were sometimes dramatically varied, people maintained a respect for individuality, even sharing a lightheartedness about it. I discovered that you can't truly learn the intricacies of anyone's deepest convictions in a passing conversation.

But even with all those differences, I found that most people value the same fundamentals in life, and I came to focus on the ninety-five percent we have in common.

I remember spending ten hours a day on the phone sometimes, just doing interviews. That was around the year I signed record deals in three territories. Having Warner Music in Canada, Rounder Records in the United States, and Greentrax Recordings in the United Kingdom felt somewhat like a dream, and it gave me a bit of muscle in the industry and some confidence to spread my wings musically. My fourth album, *No Boundaries* (1995), was the first CD I recorded after signing. I ventured out of Nova Scotia and into the big city of Toronto to collaborate with producer Chad Irschick at Inception Sound Studios.

There was a healthy budget and good support behind me, which fostered creativity and exploration of new ideas with new musicians. I was never a singer myself, but my friends Cookie Rankin of The Rankins and Bruce Guthro, who later joined Runrig, guested on a couple of vocal tracks. This was a first for me, and I used a full band with new arrangement ideas and incorporated elements of my musical tastes and those of my producer. Through all the fresh sounds, my Cape Breton style remained at the forefront and I was ready for what might come of this new blend. *No Boundaries* went on to go gold in Canada with sales exceeding 50,000 units.

Eventually, I became involved in hosting various events and awards shows, which helped me establish more relationships with industry folk and musicians alike. Children's collaborations came along too. What a blast it was to record and perform with Sharon, Lois & Bram, Raffi, and Fred Penner. Likewise, it was an honour to do guest appearances on Canada's *Sesame Park* and Britain's *Blue Peter*, the world's longest-running children's show.

On the more refined end of the spectrum, I played with some of the most beautiful orchestras throughout Canada and the United States. The Hollywood Bowl and Carnegie Hall shows were a dream. I shared the stage with Mark O'Connor, an American fiddler and friend who was one of my greatest influences, and the internationally acclaimed violinist Itzhak Perlman. I opened for Faith Hill, Don Henley, and Judy Collins, received an invitation to be a featured fiddler on *Lord of the Dance* with Michael Flatley, and toured with The Chieftains, who were so kind to also bring me along to the MusiCares Person of the Year event honouring Luciano Pavarotti in 1998. People still come up and relay how they first saw me with The Chieftains, and I'll always be tremendously grateful for the multitude of opportunities they afforded me over the years and for their irreplaceable contribution to Celtic music.

In 1997, I peaked at around 250 performances throughout Canada, the United States, the United Kingdom, Slovenia, Spain, Germany, France, Finland, Norway, Sweden, Italy, Japan, and New Zealand. All of these opportunities offered so much value for my development as a musician, as an entertainer, and as a young woman discovering the world.

Success was thrilling and a great marker for growth. I had dedicated so much to building a career and my efforts were proving effective. Even though all this meant giving up many wonderful dimensions of a normal life, the adventure was impossible to refuse.

When I attended college, I continued practicing my faith, but somewhere along the line claimed it as my own. It became less about doing church duty and more about developing a relationship with God. During this time of discovery, I was purposeful in my choice to attend Mass, and fell more deeply into my faith, gaining an intimate understanding of its value in my life.

Maintaining this dedication became a bit more challenging during my heavy touring years as I travelled to various shows, industry events, and festivals around the globe. It wasn't all work and no play. I was well rooted in my beliefs which actually provided a sort of freedom to enjoy the jams and parties, but I was no Miss Goody Two-Shoes either. Some moments carried me like a wave, and at times it was easy to have the extra drink or stay up later than I'd planned.

With late-night socializing, shows and flights, extreme touring schedules, and lots of rush and chaos, there were tempting reasons for me not to try so hard to get to Mass. In some remote locations, the church could be more than an hour away, which also made cab rides quite pricey. I even attended a Mass during an earthquake in California, which jumbled up the pay phone lines and left me with no way to get a ride back to meet the tour bus.

But I trusted and persevered, even though at times I only felt the inconvenience. I am convinced it was this focus which kept me from falling off the rails. Receiving the Eucharist really mattered to me, and if my conscience was bothered, I sought out forgiveness through confession.

When you have a real belief in something, you know what you have to do, and I was no longer just going through the motions. Rosaries, devotions, and fasting were regular in my life, and I loved drawing closer to the Lord. I developed such attentiveness for a time that every Mass moved me to tears. I treasured this gift of faith.

I also started to read Catholic books, including *Queen of the Cosmos* which became one of my favourites and eventually led me to Medjugorje, a pilgrimage site in Bosnia and Herzegovina. After I came back from Medjugorje I remember thinking, "Enough of this. Life is too short. I'm going to show my brothers how I feel." So next time I saw them, I eagerly delivered a warm embrace. It was awkward at first, but we've gone from the unhuggy types to the huggy types, and I'll take the credit for that!

When I was living with my friend Megan in an apartment in Halifax during my early twenties, I recall sitting down to read Sister Faustina's diary. As I was going through it, I became so fearful that God might have been calling me to sell all my belongings — not to be a nun or a missionary, but to change my life, to become less attached to my possessions, and to instead live more simply and prayerfully. It scared me. I just shut the book and forced myself not to think of it for a long time. But was I closing myself off to something God was calling me to do?

I remember my friend and fellow fiddler from Prince Edward Island, Bishop Faber MacDonald, telling me, "God doesn't implant deeply rooted desires in your heart unless He intends on fulfilling them." Well, selling my belongings wasn't one of my deeply rooted desires! But Bishop Faber's imparted wisdom resonated with me. I think that moment was part of the process of discerning the right call of love for my life.

In 1996, the Canadian Catholic Organization for Development and Peace invited me on a humanitarian mission. They were doing tremendous work setting up critical infrastructure in disaster-stricken areas around the world and were also working to address various social, political, and economic injustices. They were helping those living on the margins. I wanted to serve, help out in the world, and broaden my horizons.

That mission brought me to El Salvador. While the country has undergone many positive changes since I was there in the '90s, at the time there was minimal infrastructure, the education system was impoverished, crime rates were critically high mostly due to gang warfare, and homelessness and poverty were rampant.

I witnessed the very meager existence of people who did not have adequate water, food, or shelter. One of the new homes I entered, built after a hurricane destroyed the family's previous dwelling, was made of concrete blocks acquired through Development and Peace. It had a dirt floor and an opening for a window, and I thought it was hardly big enough to add a table and chairs. Meanwhile, they were all thrilled.

The locals had to deal with some pretty regressive attitudes. I met many women and heard their stories. They were often treated as objects and were neither respected nor valued.

Salvadorans lived with so little, yet they persevered courageously and with such generosity. We were welcomed into their homes and fed fresh corn tortillas that I watched them make. I did not see sorrow on their faces. I just didn't. I saw radiance and hope. Imagine that, from a poor and oppressed people. How could this be?

It caused me to ponder the very essence of life. Why were the women I met able to remain hopeful, generous, and peaceful? I really didn't know, but perhaps the less one has, the less there is to lose, and therefore the less concerned one might be about losing it. Or perhaps it was just as Mother Teresa once said, "You'll never know Jesus is all you need, until Jesus is all you have." Maybe these women had Jesus.

I felt a deep kinship with the women of El Salvador. Their beauty and strength still inspire me.

I recall saying a prayer with a friend from my group on that trip. It was a prayer within the rosary I had said my whole life, but it suddenly struck me so differently. In particular, the words "mourning and weeping in this valley of tears" stood out. I realized I hadn't yet experienced that valley of tears. I'd been blessed with an awesome life without any real suffering, and I certainly did not view life as painful. My experience in El Salvador revealed just how fortunate I had been.

Decades later, I have both seen and lived the meaning of mourning and weeping in this valley of tears. There is serious pain and suffering in the world. It is inevitable and inescapable. Regardless of our circumstances, we will all have to face heartache, illness, death, loss, fear, difficult responsibilities, and so much more. When I look back at my time in El Salvador, I am reminded that life deals its blows and yet, despite everything, life does go on. Adversity can help us understand the true and immense value of love which can sustain and conquer.

"I shouldn't be here. I want to go home. I don't know how these shows got booked. There's no time for them. I'm so mad! I don't have the energy to do this. I am so far away and I can't get home. I feel gross and lonely and tired."

I vividly recall being flopped over a wooden chair in a performance venue somewhere in England after arriving on a flight from Halifax with my band, crying on the phone to my poor mother who just took it all in. I was upset with my management, upset with my agent, and even upset with the festival for having me. I was unreasonable and inconsolable and just felt hollow in my stomach.

"Okay Nat, well go easy on yourself. You've got to try and stay positive. There are lots of good things coming up, things you're excited about. Just get through this and talk with your management about it. They'll help you to figure something out."

Although calls of this nature to my mother were rare, it wasn't the first and I needed her comfort and reassurance. Even though I argued with her, she always said what I knew deep down: that no pursuit was going to fulfill me more than music and that I needed to accept there would be trying times which would test my endurance. She provided glimmers of hope that these experiences would help me find a better balance. She was always a great listener, and I can still hear her say, as she often did, "Now, you can't just let yourself go in a pile!" And I believed her, even though I didn't admit it.

That phone call kicked off a four-week run of intense touring in the United Kingdom, followed by a day off in Canada, and then a month of performances in the United States. This had been a continuous pattern for a few years. And to top it all off, I knew this particular tour would not even pay for itself. It seemed like such a waste of energy. I grew tired of being patient and having to put on a good face week after week, month after month. I was so lonesome for home and in need of rest. I was burnt out.

Getting on the stage that night was the very last thing I wanted to do. It required great effort to stop ruminating on my negative thoughts and to ignore the pit in my stomach. Still, the show must go on, and deep down I knew darn well that my troubles were not big troubles. I tried getting in the game, did my usual warmup for an hour, put on a sparkly stage outfit, did my makeup and hair, made the set list, put my best face forward for my bandmates who I don't think were aware of my state, then drove 'er hard on the stage. My heart wasn't in it, but the show luckily brought enough positive energy to carry me through. One day at a time, right?

Thank goodness I was fortunate enough to have travelled with really amazing bandmates, in particular my friend and neighbour from Cape Breton, Mac Morin, who was always a good support when I needed it. We laughed hard through the years and he remains one of the finest people I know.

Time changes, jet lag, cancelled flights, lost luggage, no gear, little sleep, fast food or no food at all — these were trying aspects of the trenches of touring. I remember squeezing bottle caps into the rubber soles of my sneakers to mimic the tapping sounds my dance shoes would have made if only they had arrived. I broke a toe once while dancing barefoot, fell backwards over a monitor, slipped mid-performance and smashed my fiddle to pieces, did a fancy kick which split my pants from the zipper seam right up to the back waistband, vomited side stage between tunes... yes, the show did go on.

It's funny. At the times when I should have given my worst show, I was often at my best. Despite all the chaos, when the band started playing and I stood before the crowd, my blood bubbled without fail and I'd enter into a sweaty state of duty, determination, and zeal. I never doubted I'd give every last bit of me to every performance on every stage because I wanted to honour the audience, the opportunity, the talents of my band, and my role as an entertainer. On stage, there was never a shred of, "I don't care," or, "It's just one show," or, "Take it easy on yourself."

The incomparable high from an exceptional performance was a powerful fuel. But I will not deny that the awards and praise and accolades of the industry are a lovely bonus. It's instinctive to enjoy this kind of attention, but I never sought praise. In fact, I generally avoided it as my mother will attest to. I rarely read articles or reviews because I didn't want to give this awareness a dwelling in my psyche for fear I might internalize the hype and get high on my horse. Besides, an authentic Cape Bretoner would be the last to take a compliment. Being aware the praise existed was healthy affirmation, but my number one driver was making better music.

Still, I recall reading a review that did not echo the usual glowing assessment. I was probably in my mid-twenties, when things were building at a fast pace and it was difficult to keep up with the opportunities. Although I was made aware of the tone of the article, I read it anyway. Well, I discovered pretty quickly that I wasn't so tough, that I somehow must have got on a horse of some height, and that I cared rather deeply about what people thought. I felt that if I couldn't accept the criticism then I couldn't accept the praise. So, more than ever, I did not want to hear the praise. I really did not want it toying with my mind.

During a show, I learned to pay attention to what stirred me musically but also discern what my audience would really appreciate. Focusing too much on my own mood, although tempting, felt inward, while focusing too much on the crowd, although charitable, felt detached. A balance of the two was needed.

I came to recognize that there's an energy concealed in the minds and hearts of the people in the room that a performer should work to find. I tried my best to pull it out. There was a bigger picture here, which was partially about me, but more about my contribution to a greater purpose.

When I was a child, Mom often arranged for me to play some little performance for the sick and elderly, usually around Christmas or Easter. She always said, "Natalie, you'll never know how much the music means to these people." Doctors and nurses echoed the sentiment, explaining that it did more good for their patients than any drug they could offer.

The best way to understand something is to live it. I've done thousands of shows and have gone out to sign autographs after most of them. I must say, it's pretty darn stirring to hear strangers talk about some shared bond we have through the music. Comments like, "My daughter danced to your music for years," or, "I started to play fiddle because of your concert I attended when I was five," or, "I love your *No Boundaries* record. Track 10 is my favourite."

Sometimes it was more poignant. "I played your CD for my father in the hospital right up until he died. He loved your music so much. Thank you for being with us," or, "I've been battling cancer for a while and your concert tonight was a gift to me." Most of these stories came from people I'd never met.

Yet there is no doubt that I've been the one on the receiving end. I recall attending a simply stunning performance by the Kruger Brothers one evening. This trio created and delivered spectacular sounds on the banjo, guitar, bass, and vocals. Their artistic complexities, sensitivity to space, choice of harmonic progressions, and driving rhythms were so sophisticated yet playful. I was quite moved. In fact, I was so overcome with emotion that I actually started to weep.

"What breathtaking beauty," I thought, "They need to know. It's necessary that they know!" I marched on bravely and headed towards the backstage dressing rooms immediately after the show. I was a woman with a duty, responding to the moment. When I came upon the fellows and tried to express the impact of their music, ramblings sputtered through fits of sobbing. I doubt they understood any sentiments through the periodic intakes of oxygen, and I never did regain composure before realizing it was time to get out.

Then it hit me... I had become that person. You see, my reception to fans has evolved over the years. When someone used to approach me with a heartfelt story, I once thought, "Oh, okay, well that's pretty nice." It's different now, and I'm glad for that.

It's hard to put into words, but the internal expansion of my whole being that occurs during an inspirational musical moment makes me feel so rich and full of everything I need that I might burst. I now try to receive more graciously the sentiments of someone imparting their intimate feelings. I've learned to encounter them as an individual and get into their world for a bit because I can see on their face that to them, it really matters that I know.

One night in July 2000, I gave a concert on an outdoor stage at the Halifax harbour to celebrate the arrival of the Tall Ships. It was a memorable show with great attendance from locals and tourists alike. After my performance, I went to sign 8x10 photos at the autograph table. On one man's picture I wrote, "Hi William, Thanks for being here."

The profound effect this concert and inscription had on William is here for you to read in the form of the letter he wrote to me upon his return home to the United States.

Dear Natalie:

Every morning when I wake up, I thank God for you because you changed my life. In June, I was very depressed because I had lost a job. One night, I began to think about the best way to kill myself. I said to myself, "My wife will have to make the trip to Canada by herself." Immediately I realized if I was dead, she would not go by herself. So then I said, "I'll wait until we get back from Canada."

We had been planning to attend the tall ships event in Halifax, and when I saw your name on the program, I knew for sure I had to go. I had bought one of your CDs when we were in Canada the year before, but I had no idea how popular you are.

We got to the concert about an hour and a half early, but already there were no chairs left.

While we stood there waiting, I thought about my life. I have been fighting depression for a long time. When my son was very ill about ten years ago, I made a vow to stick around until he was grown. Last year he got married and moved out. Before he got sick, I had played the flute. But for ten years there had been no music in my heart, and I had not played the flute in a very long time.

When you did "In My Hands" I heard a voice say, "Go home and play." I realized then I had an instrument at home that belonged in my hands, every day.

The day after we got home I found a flute teacher and started lessons that week. I keep your picture on my music stand. You had signed it for me, "Thanks for being here." Of course, you were referring to the concert.

Now, "Thanks for being here" is my morning prayer every day. I get up at 4:00 A.M. in order to find practice time before I go to work. I have already mastered a Bach sonata, and have started on a Mozart one.

It was your music that taught my heart to sing again, and taught my feet to dance again. You are my angel who gave me the message from God that delivered me from death to life.

So every morning, for the rest of my life, I will wake up and thank God for you, and the fact that I am still here on this earth.

With deepest affection,
William

I can assure you I wasn't thinking about healing that night. I was just trying to put on a good show. What was transmitted to William goes beyond me. I believe it is God that heals an open heart in these ways. To me, stories like William's are a reflection of His love.

While compiling *In My Hands* in 1999, I was eager to add a vocal component beyond the title track. Gordie Sampson, my producer, suggested a song he wrote with Fred Lavery called "Get Me Through December." They'd written the lyrics to an old Scottish fiddle melody, "Neil Gow's Lament for the Death of his Second Wife," a beauty of a tune I'd played for years. This made the suggestion all the more meaningful. He played a demo for me and I was confident we'd found the right song.

"Yeah, I love that!"

"And who should we get to sing it?" Gordie asked.

"What about Alison Krauss?"

"Yeah, if we can get her, that would be amazing!"

"Well, I know her a little bit. I mean, we've met, and she's really lovely."

Alison had established quite a name by that time, and I honestly didn't expect she'd be able to join us on the project. Management reached out to her team and we waited for weeks, which was actually a hopeful sign since a "no" would have come quickly. The delay meant they must have been considering it. Finally, word came back that she would indeed join us on the song. We were ecstatic!

The time arrived, and our team and record label travelled to Ocean Way Nashville. Since all the pre-production was organized and had been approved by Alison, we were ready for an efficient studio session with some Nashville cats: Viktor Krauss (bass), Matt Rollings (piano), and Harry Stinson (hand drums). With me on fiddle and Gordie on guitar, we felt a powerful aura in the air. It was an incredible honour to share musical space with such highly skilled, accomplished musicians.

Alison was the coolest; sweet and chill, but focused on harnessing the depth of this song. I was in awe of her musicality and success, but even with all her accomplishments, I sensed we were driven by the same desire — to make beautiful music with incredible musicians.

Lush sounds poured from the control room speakers as we listened back to pure virtuosity. The more skilled one becomes, the more the music is able to speak and deliver a message that can move people. Alison brought sensitivity and depth to the lyrics through her interpretation, delivery, and that God-given tone which is uniquely Alison's. She is a gem in this world and I am so grateful for her.

There was no comparison between that day and my first recording session. At sixteen, I was not settled enough to think beyond the notes. I was focused on staying in tune, playing well, and not making any mistakes. When you play tunes hundreds of times over the course of years, you don't need to think so much in those ways and your mind becomes free to focus elsewhere. I learned how to find my place in a tapestry; sometimes I led and sometimes I followed. And when I found that sweet spot, the music could breathe. In there was a place for reflection and reaction. I could open, respond, and engage my heart. Sometimes I felt like I was floating. Music can become effortless.

Niel Gow's Lament for the Death of his Second Wife

Niel Gow

Get Me Through December

How pale is the sky that brings forth the rain
As the changing of seasons prepares me again
For the long bitter nights and the wild winter's day
My heart has grown cold, my love stored away
My heart has grown cold, my love stored away

I've been to the mountain left my tracks in the snow
Where souls have been lost and the walking wounded go
I've taken the pain no girl should endure
But faith can move mountains of that I am sure
Faith can move mountains of that I am sure

Get me through December
A promise I'll remember
Get me through December
So I can start again

No divine purpose brings freedom from sin
And peace is a gift that must come from within
I've looked for the love that will bring me to rest
Feeding this hunger beating strong in my chest
Feeding this hunger beating strong in my chest

Get me through December
A promise I'll remember
Get me through December
So I can start again

I've been to the mountain left my tracks in the snow
Where souls have been lost and the walking wounded go
I've taken the pain no girl should endure
But faith can move mountains of that I am sure
Faith can move mountains of that I am sure

Get me through December
A promise I'll remember
Just get me through December
So I can start again

In My Hands went on to be my best-selling recording and garnered some lovely East Coast Music Awards, a couple of Canadian Country Music Awards, and a Juno for Best Instrumental Album in 2000. Then came my first Grammy nomination that same year for my traditional recording, *My Roots Are Showing*, complete with a red carpet walk at the Staples Center in Los Angeles.

Around that time, I had a CBC special that was going to be taped in Judique, Cape Breton, and the producers wanted to focus on my family connection. This sparked in me a great duet idea with my brother Kevin. He had played fiddle and guitar for a couple of years but gave it up because he didn't like the attention. I really wanted to do this number with him so I said, "It would be amazing to have you play with me on the stage at the hall in Judique for this CBC special. What would I have to do to get you up there?"

Kevin said, "Buy me a ticket to Rome."

What a bargain! So he practiced, and we played a duo of tunes on fiddle and electric guitar. It was a dandy.

I decided to go to Italy with him, and in preparation for our big trip, Bishop Faber MacDonald worked on arranging an audience for us with Pope John Paul II. I didn't really know what that entailed, but our trip started with accommodations at the Canadian Pontifical College in Rome. We flew over in April 2000 and stayed with some awesome priests there.

When it came time for the pope's routine Wednesday Audience, Kevin and I went down to St. Peter's Basilica to attend. Thousands of people from around the globe were gathering as we walked into St. Peter's Square. We picked up our tickets, which must have been in Italian because we couldn't figure out where we were to be seated, and sought direction from one of the Swiss Guards positioned near the colonnades. When we showed him our tickets, he promptly pointed us to walk further towards the front. We walked a bit more until we met another guard, who checked the tickets and pointed us up a little further.

We kept going, but at this point Kevin and I were a bit bewildered because we were standing at the front of the entire seating arrangement. Another guard looked at our tickets and escorted us up the stairs to our seats… beside the pope's podium! We were in good company too, for there we sat amongst a hundred or so priests, nuns, bishops, and cardinals.

Looking out from that raised platform at this crowd of tens of thousands of people, we couldn't quite believe it. Then Pope John Paul II came out and sat parallel to us in his chair while he addressed this massive crowd of believers from all parts of the world.

At the end of his address, all of the clergy and nuns formed a line to greet the pope. As we approached him, I wasn't quite sure what to do. I'd seen other people kiss his ring, so I did that too and said, "Hi, Father!"

He looked me in the eye warmly and said, "I'll give you a blessing."

Kevin told me afterwards that I was supposed to call him "Your Holiness," so I'm pretty sure I messed up that part! No matter, the pope didn't seem to mind!

A few months later, I received a most wonderful invitation to host that year's Canada Day event on Parliament Hill in Ottawa for a CBC national television broadcast. In addition to hosting, they also asked me to perform. The commitment included a couple days of rehearsals beforehand.

What an amazing opportunity, and I knew it was a real honour to be involved with that show. But while I was eager to play fiddle tunes in front of a sea of people and on national television, I had already been booked in Europe for a month of performances at that time.

Well, I looked at the tour schedule, and we had a stretch of four days off after the first couple of shows in England. Those off days perfectly aligned with the Canada Day gig! I ended up travelling to Europe to do those two initial shows, flying back to Ottawa for three days to rock Parliament Hill, then back across the Atlantic to complete the rest of the European tour. It was tough but so worth it.

Oh, the adventures I obtained through the fiddle! While these might not be a big deal compared to what other, much more successful musicians could list, they are mine. Maybe I got more than I deserved or maybe less, but that's not the point. I have persevered through the decades in my career as a fiddler from Cape Breton, and I feel like I've lived nine lives already. I could never have imagined where the music would carry me.

A thrilling moment for the band and me to play live on *Late Night with Conan O'Brien*!

Mid-tour with the band in front of our bus: Matt MacIsaac, John Chaisson, me, Allan Dewar, Miche Pouliot, and Brad Davidge.

A final bow with conductor Keith Lockhart at the beautiful Symphony Hall in Boston after a memorable televised performance with the Boston Pops and Michael McDonald.

The Farmers Milk ad campaign had my picture on milk cartons.

Gold records and a Grammy nominee medal hang on the wall at Mom and Dad's home.

Performing "Get Me Through December" with Alison Krauss at the Living Arts Centre in Mississauga during my 2001 television special.

Playing an old Scottish aire atop Mount Križevac in Medjugorje.

(**ABOVE**) On stage with The Chieftains during one of their incredible American tours.

(**LEFT**) Meeting some sweet children in El Salvador during my humanitarian mission there.

Angus Young, Malcolm Young, and Phil Rudd of AC/DC with me and Pete Lespérance of Harem Scarem at a Warner Music Canada party.

Proudly holding high my first Juno Award.

A performance moment during my DVD shoot at the Celtic Colours International Festival in Cape Breton. (Photo by Eric Roth)

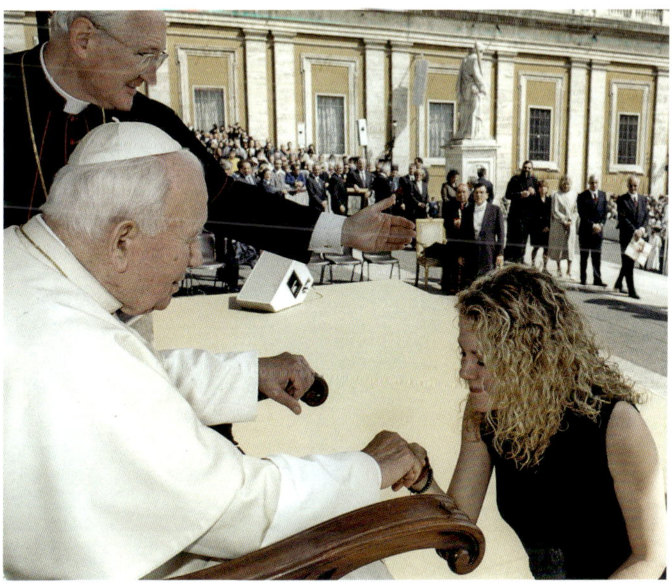

Meeting Pope John Paul II at St. Peter's Basilica in Vatican City.

Mac Morin and me on one of our many road adventures.

Donnell at a photo shoot in Toronto.
(Lisa MacIntosh Photography)

CHAPTER 4

Donnell

"Hello, Natalie. It's Donnell."

It was Easter time in 2002, and I was home from my apartment in Halifax for a few days when the phone rang. Mom answered and talked for a bit before passing it to me.

My heart skipped a beat when I heard his voice. Donnell and I had been living in separate provinces, developing our careers, travelling constantly, and dating other people. We had briefly crossed paths only three times at festivals over the last decade.

"I'm in Halifax tonight," he said, "and I was wondering if you'd like to go to dinner."

I was thrilled he'd called and immediately drove the three hours back to Halifax to meet him. We had dinner at il Mercato, a lovely restaurant I recommended, and our conversation was so enjoyable and easy that it felt like a continuation of where we had left off. In the end, we decided to meet again, and again, and then again, until we were dating once more. I was twenty-nine and Donnell was thirty-three.

This time around, it was as if a veil had been lifted. I clearly saw in him the things I'd discovered were of most value to me. Donnell was intelligent, purposeful, loyal, a man of principle, confident, charming, and witty. He was rugged yet sophisticated, dedicated to his crafts as a hardworking farmer and a phenomenally skilled fiddler, and what we shared through music was vast and unifying. And boy could he get me laughing as hard as my brothers did!

He gave the very young and the very old the same degree of interest he gave his peers. The great respect he had for his parents was obvious, and the consideration he showed my family was endearing. In public or in private, Donnell was the same man, and he earned my trust to act appropriately in any situation.

Perhaps the most telling indicator of the goodness and compatibility of our relationship was his ability to bring out the best in me. I felt inspired to be a better person while I was around him, and his actions revealed how much he cared about my life. He accommodated my commitments and encouraged my goals. Our deep conversations left me elevated, and he offered thoughtful solutions to life's curveballs. I acquired massive respect for him and came to rely on his judgement.

When Donnell and I had been dating about three weeks, the word wasn't out that we had reunited. That lasted until one day when I was visiting Donnell's place in Ontario during an unusually heavy snowfall in April and his father drove up the laneway in his truck. Frank walked into the house without a knock, then glanced at Donnell and said, "Footprints in the snow." He was referring to the two sets of tracks Donnell and I had made that led to the door.

Without pause, Frank proceeded through the house until he spied me, sitting at a desk in the office as I worked on some music. He said not a word but gently tapped a finger on his cheek a few times. Interpreting the meaning of this gesture, I stood up and gave him a kiss on the cheek. He smiled the loveliest of tender smiles, then left without a word. I was proud to know Donnell's wise and loving father approved of me.

After about a month of dating this second time, I asked Donnell to join me on a special trip to Orlando, Florida, with the Children's Miracle Network, for whom I was a spokesperson that year. It was a real privilege to be with those sweet children for a week as they bravely fought their illnesses with such grace. Beauties, every one of them.

One Saturday night in Florida, after a full day of ceremonies and obligations, Donnell and I attended an evening Mass. An exceptional church choir sang "Panis

Angelicus" while I walked up to the altar and received the Host. Returning to my pew, I glanced up for a moment to behold the most magnificent orange moon hanging in the church entrance. The double doors had been left wide open, the moon had risen to just the perfect spot, and tears flowed while I witnessed this incredible culmination of nature, music, love, and God.

We dined at a very high-end restaurant that night after Mass. The sommelier expertly poured us a matching wine for each course and our conversation flowed just as smoothly. We got to talking about Cape Breton and how wonderful it was, but I let Donnell know I would leave there if I had to. I told him, "Wherever my life makes sense, all things considered."

He got the message; I was ready to commit. I was deeply invested and had determined in my heart that I would never lose Donnell again.

I had come to recognize that Donnell was rare and our bond was beautiful and unique. My love transitioned from, "Oh this is really fun and I am excited to be with you," to a conviction that Donnell was the best person in whom to invest my love. Perhaps that sounds coldly calculated or lacking the magic attraction found in the movies. But love is the greatest gift we have to give, so I wanted to be sure I'd found the best person for my lifelong commitment. My will ignited, and I thanked God every day for this second chance.

A couple of weeks later, in May 2002, I went to the Halifax airport to pick up Donnell for a weekend visit. We headed out to Cape Breton after a quick stop where I showed him the new condo unit I had purchased six months prior. Construction was well underway, and it had progressed to the point where I was choosing flooring, paint, and appliances. I'd had the walls soundproofed, and my unit was on the ground level at the end of the hall with only a parking garage underneath. It was thrilling to have a place where I could practice and pound my foot without disturbing anyone. I remember asking Donnell's opinion about range hoods so he could help me decide the best option because the builders needed to know what to install. It seemed so important at the time.

When we got on the road to Cape Breton, Donnell suggested we drop in to see Mary and Peter, Donnell's cousin, after a visit with Mom and Dad. My parents always thought a lot of Donnell. There were so many great connections for them: our mothers had danced and performed in many of the same local events during their youth, my parents grew up on farms and in large families just like Donnell, and we all held so much in common through our Catholic faith. Then of course there was the fiddling. Mom and Dad loved fiddle music more than almost anything, and they were quite proud of Donnell's accomplishments.

After a quick visit home, we set off again for Mary and Peter's place. On the way, Donnell suggested we make a brief detour over to his mom's parish in Broad Cove. I thought it was a pretty cool idea, especially since it involved a charming drive down a back road.

Donnell parked the car at the church, and I followed him to the graveyard where he visited his grandparents' resting place. What a sweet thing to do. It was a rainy late afternoon, and I noticed Donnell getting slightly emotional standing above his grandfather's grave. He motioned for me to follow him into the church where we knelt down to pray. I closed my eyes and felt the spirituality of the moment. Donnell connected so deeply to his ancestry, his people, and his Cape Breton roots. And there I was, praying beside him in this church where his mom used to pray as a little girl.

Just before we walked out the door, Donnell turned to me and said, "Nat, there's something else."

The intense look on his face was like nothing I had seen before, and I actually braced myself for the worst. What did he have to tell me? In this split second, I knew confidently that no matter what he had to say, I would be strong and love him through this moment however I could. I felt a sort of courage fill me as I prepared myself.

He knelt down on one knee and pulled a small box out from his jacket pocket. As he opened it, I saw the ring.

"Will you marry me?" he asked.

After a brief moment of shock, I exclaimed, "Yes, I will!"

What a curveball! I honestly thought I was going to be dealing with some heavy burden. We were both shaking and couldn't stop giggling like little kids.

We never did go to Mary and Peter's house. Turns out he'd never planned to take me there anyway. And I never made a decision about that range hood. Imagine what he must have been thinking, knowing he was going to propose while I was rambling on about a range hood in a condo he knew I'd probably never set foot in. And I never did. We still joke about it to this day.

Anyone who has experienced a proposal knows the thrill of sharing this juicy secret with family and friends. It is one of life's most exhilarating moments. But how disappointing to come back to an empty house and wait over an hour for my parents' return. They were surprised to see we hadn't gone to visit Mary and Peter. We got to chatting in the kitchen and I sat purposely upright with my fingers spread out across my lap to draw attention to my new piece of jewellery. I kept waving my hands and wiggling my fingers until Mom finally noticed the ring.

But my parents were surprisingly calm. What I didn't know was that Donnell had gone out to the garage with my dad that afternoon and asked him for his blessing to marry me. Dad gave Donnell his full support, and then Dad of course told Mom, so they were expecting the news at some point. I guess I wasn't the first to know!

I believe getting that second chance was an answer to my mother's ceaseless prayers that I would find a good man. She divulged much later that she had prayed for years, "Dear God, give Natalie a good fellow like St. Joseph."

Donnell and I joke about that all the time. Something will come up and I'll say to him, "Yeah, you're not like St. Joseph now!"

I knew that my prayers for the right person had been answered too. Donnell's parents had a lot to do with that since they poured so much of themselves into his formation. I was the lucky recipient of all their efforts.

Anticipating our life together, I wondered about Donnell's needs. I desired to help him flourish in life and to help lead him to Heaven. I trusted I'd find a way, just as love had found a way and brought us together. It inspired me to write this poem:

As rain falls from the sky
And water fills the sea,
As a mountain does stand tall
Just trust in love, believe.

As the bee will find her flower
And the rising sun is true,
Love will find a way,
It led me here to you.
Oh, love will find a way,
It led me here to you.

Like many engaged couples, we took part in a marriage preparation course before our wedding. Donnell and I were pretty confident about our compatibility. We had the same views on everything: faith, family, music, culture, work, money, career, and our shared future.

During that marriage course, we were introduced to natural family planning, which I found fascinating. Those sessions taught me more about my body than my twelve years of health and science classes combined! I was keen to absorb the information from those rich conversations, despite the fact that at times I squirmed in my seat as I divulged aloud my intimate reproductive details to Donnell and our NaPro consultant.

Among the many exercises of the program, each couple was asked to discuss children in private, specifically how many they wanted. I've always loved babies right from the time I was a toddler. Seeing the effect they had on people, but especially on my mom, was a stunning sight. Watching her with a baby had me convinced this was the most special thing in the world. It was love in plain sight and so attractive to me.

I was pretty confident that Donnell knew my attitude about babies and I knew his. We both wanted a family. Given that we were thirty and thirty-four, and assuming we might have a child every couple of years, we calculated we might have four or five children. We discovered we had a similar, flexible attitude about being open to what life had to offer, and although we weren't the types to abandon logic and reasoning, we considered God a part of our marriage and had an attitude of cooperation with His plan.

October 5, 2002, was the greatest day of my life. Donnell and I were joined in the union of marriage in a beautiful and traditional wedding ceremony before all of our family and friends at Stella Maris Parish, the church of my childhood in Creignish, Cape Breton.

Guests were greeted by the sound of bagpipes played by my longtime bandmate Matt MacIsaac until the day's blustery weather forced him inside. While the rain had stopped by the time my parents and I arrived at two o'clock, Tina MacMaster, my matron of honour and sister-in-law, had to hold the train of my strapless gown so it wasn't caught by the wind.

There's no doubt that the butterflies in my stomach were in full flight that day. But as I approached the altar, I caught sight of Donnell. I steadied. Here was my anchor. That feeling of determination I experienced in the moments before he proposed consumed me once again.

It was my trust in God that led me to the altar with this man, and I wanted to give back every bit of gratitude to my Father in Heaven for the gift that stood before me. I felt like the luckiest woman in the world. Nothing could have mattered more, and nothing could shake my conviction in our union.

I entered deeply into the Mass and absorbed the meaning of it all. Hymns like "Jesu, Joy of Man's Desiring" and "Prayer of St. Francis" carried much meaning for us and were sung beautifully by Donnell's sisters and my extended family. Our fiddler friend Mark O'Connor played a beautiful waltz during the Mass as well, and all my fiddling relatives played us out the door with a lively tune. Father Hughie married us while Bishop Faber MacDonald delivered a very meaningful homily which he copied for me and I still refer to from time to time. In it, Bishop Faber quoted an expression Father John Angus Rankin used: "Two things in this world are eternal: music and love."

Afterwards, we held a reception at the Judique Community Centre. We feasted on seafood, beef, chicken, and every possible side dish, all prepared by Donnell's cousin, Chef Daryl MacDonnell. Drinks were flowing and desserts continued right through the night. It was indeed a party and truly felt like a ripper of a traditional Cape Breton wedding. There were speeches, a live band, guest fiddlers, square sets, and lots of dancing. We did the traditional wedding party dances of father-daughter and mother-son. Donnell and I danced our first waltz to "Some Day My Prince Will Come." Everyone was so generous and kind and sincerely enthusiastic.

An amusing anecdote to share: I realized two days before the wedding that Donnell and I had neglected to prepare a gift for each of our wedding guests. "What will we do, Donnell? How can we give something meaningful this late in the game?"

Donnell said almost instantly, "No problem, Nat. We will just write them a tune."

Over the next hour or so we dove in. I wrote the first part and Donnell wrote the second part. We called it "Wedding Day Jig." I transcribed the melody by hand onto manuscript paper as best I could, then booted 'er up to Port Hawkesbury to get 500 copies made. I picked them up the next day and rolled them into cute scrolls tied with red ribbons. That was the first piece of music we wrote together.

Wedding Day Jig

Natalie MacMaster and Donnell Leahy

"This travelling bachelorette lifestyle needs a makeover!" I thought, as I stood in our kitchen in Ontario.

At thirty, my culinary repertoire was extremely lacking. I could keep Donnell and myself alive, but that was about it. During my intensely busy twenties, I lived in my apartment for only one or two months each year. There was never a need nor the time to learn how to prepare nice dinners, so I just cooked basics like frozen fries, pan-fried chicken breasts, or Kraft Dinner (which I still love).

I was very aware of the new role I'd taken on in life, and I was eager to become what I needed to be, no matter what that meant. My mom was always such a great cook, and I suppose I wanted to be like her, but I didn't recognize it as such. Who says they want to be like their mother? Usually it's the opposite, and that's no insult because despite all the inspiring mothers out there, don't we all just want to do life our own way? But I'll tell you, Mom is now my gold standard.

She always took care of people and things. From cooking and cleaning to revamping and redesigning, from renovating the tiniest detail to making the grandest overhaul, adjustments were made to every room of my childhood Cape Breton dwelling. Through all of her efforts, Mom made our house beautiful, gave it heart, and made it a home. I wanted to do the same. It seemed natural to immerse myself in painting and matching, placing things here and there, moving and removing, and shopping for what we needed. It was mostly fun, and Donnell was mostly a yes-man. I continue to discover the power of decor which is never to be underestimated.

I embarked with great enthusiasm on a journey to become a more sophisticated cook. This worked well with our newly married balance since Donnell had no interest in cooking whatsoever. He was out the door early in the morning, farming all day on a family property a few miles away. I was happy to take this on and could see that our roles were naturally starting to define themselves. Mind you, he has cooked me many a fine steak and potato dinner.

I remember attending a potluck and following a recipe from a book for the very first time. That ginger chicken recipe was my introduction to a whole new way of cooking. Every meal became an adventure. We ate sumptuously for weeks, drank fine wine with supper, and never rushed the experience. I was in control here, delighted with my elaborate menu planning. In fact, I came to enjoy cooking so much as a newlywed that it developed into a passion. With a bit of practice, anyone can do this!

A couple of months after getting married, armed with my newly discovered zeal for cooking and a slightly expanded culinary repertoire, I had the bright idea to invite my in-laws to our house for dinner.

My parents had visited about a month before that planned dinner. Mom, in her usual proactive manner, decided to do some grocery shopping for me so I would have a good selection of staples in my pantry. Among other things, she made a trip to the bulk store and purchased a number of baking items contained in clear plastic bags. I was quite happy to have my pantry closet looking so well stocked.

I was especially excited about making a German apple cake for dessert. I knew this was a guaranteed "knock your socks off" type of dessert because my Aunt Mary Janet told me so. Although I'd never made this particular cake before, the recipe came from Mary Lorette Beaton, one of Cape Breton's finest bakers. With confidence inspired by these two ladies, I was sure the cake would be a hit.

I dove into the project with great enthusiasm. I called Mom a couple times to ensure I was doing things correctly. In particular, I thought the batter had a strange consistency. Nevertheless, I poured the batter into the cake tin and set the oven to 350°F.

I called Mom a minute or two later. "Is it normal for this cake to rise so quickly? It's only been in the oven a few minutes and it's almost dripping over the side of the cake pan."

She said that it would probably stop rising and it should be fine. And then came my next call where I exclaimed, "Mom, this thing has only been in a couple more minutes and it's dripping all over the oven floor! It just won't stop rising!"

I watched my cake grow and grow and grow to the point where I knew something was greatly amiss. I removed it from the oven, dumped it into a fresh garbage bag, and set it at the door for Donnell to take out. But wait… the cake batter was still growing! I stood by and watched the bag double in size! Would this German apple cake take over the whole house?

Eventually, the culprit was revealed. The bags of baking ingredients Mom stashed in my pantry were unmarked. The recipe called for two cups of flour, but I'd put in two cups of baking powder instead. That oughta do it!

In 1998, while in town for a show with the Edmonton Symphony Orchestra, I stayed at Hotel Macdonald and tried sticky toffee pudding for the first time. I asked the chef for the recipe as I could not believe how good this dessert was.

Sticky toffee pudding has now become Donnell's absolute favourite dessert. I make it for every birthday, Christmas, Easter, guest dinner, and when I want to do something thoughtful for him. You'd think he'd be sick of it by now, but no! The recipe below is one that I switched over to a few years ago. It's a bit easier to prepare than the Hotel Macdonald version and it tastes just as good.

Oh, to think back to the days when it was just the two of us! As far away as that time now seems, I can return to those blissful moments when we dreamed our dreams, made a home, and took a much-needed break.

The dirt road Donnell and I lived on during our first six years of marriage was my first experience of living in Ontario. We had a sweet, little brick bungalow complete with local vegetation planted by the previous residents. I was grateful for these gardens because my thumb was as far from green as ever there was. I didn't even know that pulling weeds was an ongoing thing! Needless to say, the previously manicured plant life became lush with extra greenery. But I thought some of the weeds were kind of pretty, which gave me a good excuse to just leave them there. Donnell never seemed to mind.

I remember one night early in our marriage when we went to a party at a friend's place. On the car ride home, I declared to Donnell, "Well, that was lame!"

I believe it was the first time I'd been to a party with no live music. Imagine that! This discovery revealed there were some pretty cool things about being raised in Cape Breton.

My first Ontario winter made me think I was living in some kind of wonderland. I came from the capital of blustery winters where wild gusts of hail and freezing rain created treacherous driving conditions on narrow, winding roads. Here, protected by an enclave of trees on our one-acre property, the winter wind vanished and the trees just sat still, looking so picturesque with snow-covered, pillowy branches. It was a completely different experience, like something out of a fairy tale.

With all my travels, I had become somewhat of a vagabond, unattached to any type of landscape. For this reason, I never anticipated any problem with my relocation to Ontario. And despite what I was told would likely happen, I didn't miss the ocean. With all this new beauty surrounding me — rolling farm fields, attractive trees, sprawling countryside, fresh spring grass, and foliage arriving two weeks earlier than back home — I figured I was just going from one charming place to another.

Months passed, and one day I went for a walk down our dirt road. I meandered along pastures and greenery, and for the first time in my life, I experienced a claustrophobia of sorts.

"Where does this end?" I thought. "Where is the edge of the earth? I can't get to the edge."

I was inland. Far inland. A feeling of entrapment and a longing to reach the ocean just hit me. I didn't need to know north, south, east, or west; I just needed to know where the ocean was. It unknowingly provided me with a sense of place, and it was so strange to discover the absence of that majestic body of water. It was a feeling I thought this tough ol' travelled gal could never have experienced, but I did, and I felt part of the community of East Coasters missing their beloved ocean.

After a few wonderful months of marriage, Donnell and I decided it was time to put some focus on starting a family. With this intent, a whole year passed and… nothing. Something wasn't right. This triggered a visit to the St. Marguerite Bourgeoys Fertility*Care* centre in Toronto. The attention we received there from Dr. Julia, a NaPro specialist, was sincerely caring and diligent, and much time was spent weeding out possible causes of infertility. There were no quick and clear answers, and we considered seriously for the first time that perhaps we would not be able to have children. It was so disheartening. Donnell was deflated as well, although we weren't the types to open up too much about things that weighed each other down. We spoke a little about adoption but didn't think that was a decision to be made so early.

We focused on the purpose of our marriage and its unique journey, desiring to be willing participants in this love story no matter the outcome. But even with that mindset, I let myself wonder, "Is there something wrong with me? Maybe I'm unable to have children." The thought of not becoming a mother wasn't as difficult as the thought of me being the reason for Donnell not becoming a father.

That was a time when I better understood the words of Mother Teresa, "You'll never know Jesus is all you need until Jesus is all you have." I embarked on a much healthier prayer life. I took walks and cried and talked to God. I said to Him, "Donnell and I would make good parents, wouldn't we? Look at all those unwanted babies, and here we are established and ready for any of them. Why are you not giving us one?"

I was never as close to God as I was then. Even though my heart broke every month, I still felt hope for something and so I prayed, a lot. I said novenas, and Donnell and I prayed together.

In April 2004, I chose a five-day novena to St. Thérèse of Lisieux and asked her to pray with me that God would help us conceive a child by the end of the year. In St. Thérèse's spiritual autobiography, *Story of a Soul*, she claimed she would continue her prayers for souls after her death and send forth a shower of roses from Heaven to Earth. It is believed that if your request is to be granted, you will receive roses in some form.

Now, keep in mind that although I am a woman of faith, I do realize how ridiculous this may sound. If you don't share my faith, bear with me. It's a great story and one of many about roses I have received during novenas to St. Thérèse over the past thirty years.

On the eve of the fifth day of that April novena, my friend Barbara came over to visit. Unaware of my petition to St. Thérèse, she surprised me with a bouquet of roses. I remained calm, but after she left I was jumping for joy! Unexpected roses! I was going to get pregnant, I was sure of it.

But then life went on and on and on. By October I was quite discouraged, and when December arrived with no baby news I was so disappointed. I just couldn't figure it out, it was supposed to have happened by now. More prayers ensued, and my doctor continued testing for various things. Eventually, she discovered that I had low progesterone and advised that it could be helpful to start giving myself injections of hCG (human chorionic gonadotropin), a hormone produced by the placenta crucial during the early phases of pregnancy.

A few months into 2005, I arrived back from a tour to find spring in the air, and I headed to the grocery store for some ingredients to make a nice supper. I decided to buy a spring flower bouquet while at the checkout, which is something I never did. In fact, I think that was the first time I'd ever bought myself flowers.

When I returned home and was unpacking the bags, I pulled out my little bouquet to trim the bottoms and arrange them in a vase on the kitchen table. They gave our house an extra homey feel. We had a lovely meal and I was happy to be with Donnell again.

The next day when I was wiping the table, I noticed that the bouquet included some tiny yellow baby roses. Roses. Roses? Oh my gosh, yes, ROSES! Only a few days before I had started another novena to St. Thérèse for the same intention. Now I was trembling.

Donnell was out farming and I didn't want to tell him over the phone. When he arrived home a couple of hours later, I showed him the three small baby roses hidden amongst the lilies and greenery. He shrugged and told me that they didn't count because I bought them myself. "You can't answer your own novena, Nat," he stated matter-of-factly.

Really? He thought I bought myself roses to answer my own prayer?

"Donnell, I didn't know they were in there," I replied. "I didn't see them when I bought the bouquet, and I didn't even notice them until today!"

"Well, okay," he said, but it was apparent he didn't share my excitement. I, on the other hand, was confident something incredible was going to happen. I just didn't know when.

A few days after the discovery of the roses in our kitchen table bouquet, I was off again doing some shows in the United States. Donnell and I had not yet amalgamated our performance careers, and everywhere I played it was just me and my band.

I had a call scheduled with my doctor while at a venue a few days into the tour. After some discussion and consideration of her calculations, she suggested I have blood work done to see if I was pregnant. This was the first time she had ever suggested I do this, but I knew better than to get my hopes up.

A couple of days later, while in an odd basement of the theatre we were playing that night, my phone rang. It was Dr. Julia again. "Congratulations, Natalie! I'm looking at your blood test results here, and you are indeed pregnant!"

"Are you serious?" I exclaimed, in shock. I could feel the blood rippling up through my body like fireworks and I was trembling with excitement. "Are you serious?"

"Yes, of course," she replied.

I tried to remain calm, aware I was talking to someone I didn't know all that well. Though, in that moment, it seemed she knew me better than anyone.

"Oh my God, oh my God! Oh! This is unbelievable!" I said, my voice loud and high-pitched, filled with enthusiasm and happiness of the greatest magnitude.

“That is the best response I’ve ever heard,” said Dr. Julia, and we had a great chuckle.

“Well, I have to go and call Donnell!” I said excitedly, rushing to get off the phone. “Thank you so much for everything, Dr. Julia. This is INCREDIBLE!”

I was shaking and bursting with emotion as I tried dialling Donnell’s number. I’m surprised I didn’t pass out with the intensity.

“Hello?”

“Donnell, I’m pregnant!”

Silence. He whispered, “Are you serious? Nat, are you serious?”

“YES!” I screamed.

“Nat, oh my God. Are you serious, Nat?”

I screamed again, “YES!”

“Can I swear?” he asked, and then he did, and we giggled with a joy beyond any we’ve ever experienced.

We were both in tears, awestruck at this discovery. I was overflowing with gratitude on that day. Our journey to this point had seemed so long and disappointing, and despite my hope through it all, there were some very tough moments trying to accept that we might not be able to have children. All the hope in the world does not take away one’s human tendencies.

We realized then that it was just under a year from the time I had started that original novena. While I had pegged December as the end of the year, technically, it was April! We thanked God over and over. I was so immensely full of gratitude, I had it in my head that even if my baby didn’t make it to birth, I was now and always would be, a mother.

Chicken in Ginger Sauce

Total time: 40 minutes   *Serves: 4*

INGREDIENTS

4 (6-oz.) boneless, skinless chicken breasts
2 tbsp vegetable oil
6 green onions, finely chopped
3 garlic cloves, finely chopped
1 piece fresh ginger root (2-inch), peeled and grated
1 tsp ground cumin
2 tsp garam masala
Salt and pepper to taste
1 tbsp lemon juice
6 tbsp hot water
Parsley sprigs and lemon slices to garnish

METHOD

1. Rinse the chicken breasts and pat dry with paper towels. Then, slice each chicken breast into quarters.
2. Heat oil in a large skillet, adding chopped onions. Cook on medium-high heat, stirring constantly until softened, about 3 minutes. Remove fried onions with a slotted spoon.
3. Add the sliced chicken to the skillet and cook over medium-high heat for about 5 minutes, or until nicely browned on both sides.
4. Stir in garlic, ginger root, cumin, garam masala, salt, and pepper, cooking for 1 minute.
5. Add the fried onions, lemon juice, and water, then cover and cook over medium-low heat for 10-12 minutes, or until chicken is tender and cooked through.
6. Serve hot over rice and garnish with chopped parsley and lemon slices.

Sticky Toffee Pudding

Total time: 1 hour and 10 minutes   *Serves: 8*

PUDDING

INGREDIENTS

1⅓ cups water
1⅓ cups seeded dates, coarsely chopped
1 tsp baking soda
⅓ cup softened butter
¾ cup brown sugar, packed
2 large eggs
1 cup all-purpose flour
2 tsp baking powder
1 tsp ground cinnamon

METHOD

1. Preheat oven to 350°F (180°C).
2. Bring the water to a boil. Add the dates and stir. Then, reduce temperature to medium and allow to continue boiling without stirring for about 5 minutes.
3. Remove from heat and add the baking soda. Stir then set to the side.
4. In a large bowl, cream the butter and sugar. Add the eggs, flour, baking powder, cinnamon, and date mixture, incorporating well.
5. Pour into a greased 8-inch springform pan. Bake in the oven for 50-55 minutes or until a toothpick inserted in the centre comes out clean.

WARM CARAMEL SAUCE

INGREDIENTS

½ cup heavy whipping cream
½ cup butter
½ cup brown sugar, packed

METHOD

1. Combine the ingredients in a saucepan.
2. Bring to a boil. Reduce temperature to medium and allow to continue boiling without stirring for about 5 minutes.
3. Remove from heat and stir until smooth. Pour warm sauce over individual slices to serve.

German Apple Cake

Total time: 2 hours *Serves: 10*

CAKE BASE

INGREDIENTS

3 large eggs
1 cup oil (any kind)
2 cups white sugar
1 tsp vanilla
2 cups all-purpose flour
2 tsp cinnamon
1 tsp baking soda
1 tsp mace (omit if you have none)
1 cup raisins, big sticky ones preferably
3 large or 4 small Granny Smith apples, peeled and sliced

METHOD

1. In a bowl, whisk together the eggs, oil, sugar, and vanilla.
2. In a separate bowl, mix together the flour, cinnamon, baking soda, and mace.
3. Stir dry ingredients into wet ingredients, adding raisins and apples.
4. Pour into a greased and floured 9-inch springform pan.
5. Bake at 350°F (180°C) for 55-60 minutes. While the cake is baking, mix the cream cheese topping.

CREAM CHEESE TOPPING

INGREDIENTS

1 250-gram block of cream cheese, softened
2 tbsp butter, softened
2 tsp vanilla
2 cups icing sugar
Pinch of salt

METHOD

1. Mix all ingredients together in a bowl until smooth and creamy.
2. Remove the cake from oven when done and pour the cream cheese topping evenly over the hot cake.
3. Return the cake to oven for 20 minutes more or until the top is lightly browned and caramelized.
4. Remove the cake from oven and allow to cool.
5. Slide a knife around the edge of the springform pan to unstick the sides before opening the spring lock.
6. Slice in wedges and serve with a dollop of real whipped cream.

Donnell just before heading to the church for our wedding.

Me, moments after getting married.

(LEFT) Donnell and I stand proudly at the altar with our parents, Alex, Minnie, Julie, and Frank.

(BELOW) A sweet father-daughter moment in the kitchen, just before heading out the door to be married.

(LEFT) Overcome with the deeper meaning of our wedding ceremony.

Delighted with my new adventure of performing while pregnant.

CHAPTER 5

A New Balance

As I pondered how life might change with a newborn baby, I guessed I would stay home to raise our little one. In fact, I assumed before even discussing it with Donnell that being a mother would require me to leave most of my career. Sure, I imagined I'd still play music, but I thought my growth and development would pause and that I would need to give up touring. Not just for a few months, but indefinitely.

But instead of watching me shut that door, Donnell encouraged me to open it wider. He said simply, "You won't know what this will be like until you try, Nat." His support was pivotal and sweetly empowering. He believed in me and my music and endorsed the continuation of my passion. Donnell's love is really the reason this book is in your hands. If he had doubted me or reserved encouragement, I would've cancelled my shows to slow down significantly. Instead, I donned a new title — a stay-at-home mom on the road!

Having Mary Frances was the most amazing dream come true. She was born in December 2005 and named after my mother and Donnell's father. We were finally able to hold our own beautiful baby, and I felt as though no one in the world was ever more thrilled. We marvelled at her sweet little face, long fingers, itty-bitty toenails, detailed ears, and that tuft of hair which stood straight up at all times. Watching her squirm or yawn or just breathe was absolutely fascinating. Dressing her up in so many of the beautiful outfits we had received over the past six months was a delight in itself. Mind you, she'd sometimes go through four a day, the messy little thing that she was.

Even with all of that wonder and joy, the adjustment felt much bigger than I ever could have imagined, despite what everyone tried to prepare me for. Perhaps I should have clued in, given that at thirty-three I had never even changed a diaper.

Shortly after childbirth, I was thrust into nursing. Now who would ever think that something as natural as baby to breast would be such a complex maneuver? This latching was incredibly difficult and painful for the first couple of weeks. I'd heard that could happen for some women, but this was beyond my imagination.

It slowly got easier over the following days, and I eventually mastered the technique, which became effortless and comfortable after about three weeks. It didn't feel like there was much time to get things done between feedings, and I often had to choose between sleeping, eating, or showering. Mary Frances slept a lot but not for long stretches. When she awoke in the middle of a nap, I did not expect how tough it would be to get her settled again. It often required a lot of rocking or bouncing or pacing. My arms were tired all the time!

In fact, I remember when Mary Frances was just a couple weeks old and we were trying to lull her back to sleep in the wee hours of the morning. I was sitting on the couch with Donnell and proclaimed through the tears, "I don't know if I'll ever laugh again." It seems so comical to me now.

Five weeks passed quickly, and then came time to try out my first round of touring and performing as a new mother. I couldn't help but wonder if I'd be less than I was before. Would I get out of breath dancing? Would I look stage-ready with my new body? Would I be able to play well having had less practice time? I dreaded letting down a crowd.

That first moment walking out to greet the audience was such a surprise for me. I transformed back into the old, familiar Natalie, doing the same things I had done for twenty-three years before this massive new change. My band was groovin' out while Mom stood side stage with my delicate newborn in her capable arms.

The familiar rush of adrenaline felt like an old friend, and the connection I made with the audience gave me confidence that maybe I could be a mom and continue performing. Dancing post-pregnancy was a breeze compared to dancing while seven months pregnant. I even forgot I was a mother at one point! Didn't see that coming!

Those moments on stage were electrifying. Can you believe that performing became a break for me? Well, I wasn't looking for a break, but boy it refreshed me better than any spa treatment ever could! When the performance was over and I went back to my baby in her Gramma's arms, I found a new kind of sweetness in those warm, cuddly snuggles.

I remember one particular night when I was about to go to sleep with Mary Frances beside me in a crib. She kept squirming and making her little whimpers.

"What could be wrong?" I thought. "It's eleven o'clock. She should be ready to sleep." I had changed her, fed her, and burped her, but she still wasn't settling.

Mom offered, "Let me take Mary Frances and I'll rock her to sleep."

I went out like a light but awoke at around four a.m. in a panic. "How come Mary Frances didn't wake up?" I thought. "She wakes up every couple of hours!" I looked in the crib but it was bare.

I went into the other room and there was my mother, still awake in a chair, holding her granddaughter. She'd been there for five hours, rocking my baby, just so I could get some sleep.

By the end of 2006, I'd travelled to do about a hundred shows. Mary Frances was with me for all of them. My mom was there for quite a few and Aunt Mary Janet helped out with some as well. A family friend, Tony Butcher, assisted with logistics and has reliably supported us for over eighteen years. As well, Dianne Fitzpatrick has been an incredible asset to our operation for more than three decades and worked diligently in various capacities behind the scenes. Through the years, I've received huge help for a variety of needs from many spectacular people within our community. I just could not have done what I did without them.

That year, my management office received a most wonderful call notifying us that I had been awarded the Order of Canada. While that was certainly not something I ever expected, it was a great honour to be recognized by my country in that way. Donnell, Mary Frances, and my mom and dad were all there for the grand investiture ceremony at Rideau Hall in Ottawa in May 2007. Someone else was there too… I was seven months pregnant with our second child.

We welcomed our boy Michael into the world in June 2007. He was named after the first Leahy ancestor to arrive in Canada from Ireland in 1825. At thirty-five, I was so thrilled to have both a daughter and a son.

One thing that became quite clear to me over the next few years was that this little boy was very different from his sister. While Mary Frances could sit for hours crafting, colouring, or looking at books, Michael couldn't sit for a minute. He was physical. While Mary Frances contentedly played, Michael aggressively explored. This little guy would run all day long and still have the energy to do it all over again. I can picture the intensity with which he rode the hobby horse I had made for him. He believed he was a real cowboy with real tasks both outside and inside the house, up the stairs and down. Face beet red, eyes wide, and stone serious, he galloped everywhere, focused on his duties. By the end of a good long ride, he'd be sweating all over. I think he rode that horse every day for ten years.

After marrying Donnell, I was often asked, "How does it feel to become part of such a large family?"

My answer was usually, "The same."

While Donnell is one of eleven siblings and I'm one of just three, I oddly never noticed any major differences, which I'm sure was due to the many extended family gatherings I attended growing up. My life was often consumed with cousins and aunts and uncles. But I will say, one effect of Donnell having so many siblings was that his pranks often came back to bite us in surprising ways.

As a gift to Mary Frances at her fourth birthday party, Donnell's oldest sister, Chrissy, plunked down a Coors Light box in the middle of our living room floor. That box began to wiggle, and within seconds a darling puppy poked out its head!

So cute, but really? Mary Frances was immediately smitten with this fluffy, white sheepdog whom she named Paul. Donnell scowled at his sister, who promptly reminded him of the time her firstborn, Brendan, turned four, and Donnell had surprised him with a baby rabbit. She had been waiting all this time to return the favour.

Mary Frances didn't notice any other gift for the rest of the night. She had Paul and that's all that mattered. But Donnell and I knew that we could not keep the puppy with our touring schedule. The dog would have to go elsewhere, there was no way around it. We found Paul a wonderful new home with a friend, but as you can imagine, Mary Frances was pretty heartbroken. This awakened in her a determination to get a dog. She would go on to pray for a dog every morning and evening, during every grace, at every meal, every day… for five years!

Although this had its persuasive effect on us, Donnell and I were just not equipped to have a dog. We were not living in our forever home, and explained to Mary Frances that once our new home was constructed, there would be a better setup for a dog, at which point we would get her one.

I didn't grow up with any animals, not even a goldfish, so the concept of actually owning a dog was slightly terrifying. I'd always been afraid of them. As Mary Frances got older, she figured out my distaste for dogs and discovered I was praying we *wouldn't* get one. She'd poke fun at me and say, "Let's see who He listens to!"

We now have two dogs, five horses, ten laying hens, and a multitude of bunnies in our backyard. I've come a long way. It's amazing what can be acquired when you find the sweet spot between order and chaos.

In February 2009, our dear Clare was born and given a family name we had always loved. From her first arrival into our lives, Clare was the quirky one. She was similar to Mary Frances in that she too could while away the hours quietly focused on something, but her inquisitive nature inclined her towards mischief.

On one occasion when Donnell and I were heading to a friend's party with two other couples, we had all decided to meet at our place and then drive over together.

The babysitter arrived a few minutes early and was nicely settled in to take care of our children. Then our friends showed up, and through enthusiastic chatter we loaded the trunk with platters of sweets and charcuterie. Donnell and I said our goodbyes and shut the door, exuberantly savouring the feeling of freedom and a night out with friends.

The twenty-minute ride to the party was a hoot. Lots of girly talk, loose chit-chat, and a few good laughs on the way. When we arrived at our destination and piled out of the van, I went around to the back to get the food. As I opened the trunk door I heard, “Surprise!” It was four-year-old Clare who bounced up, arms stretched high with enthusiasm.

“Clare! What are you doing in there?” I exclaimed.

Donnell immediately phoned the babysitter who had been looking for our daughter and was rightly in a panic. Donnell gave Clare a stern talking to during the immediate drive back home, while the rest of us went into the party chuckling about her antics. She still manages to find ways to surprise us.

Our first few years with children involved pretty hectic touring schedules. Donnell had shows with Leahy, his renamed family band, that has performed nationally and internationally since the 1980s, and we were often on separate tours. While I usually had the children, sometimes Donnell took along one or two if it made sense. We always imagined that some form of musical amalgamation was inevitable, but it took a while for that to become a reality.

I recall a conversation I had with Donnell’s father one time. I was in Winnipeg performing with the Winnipeg Symphony Orchestra. I phoned Frank after the show to discuss details, a habit he insisted on no matter what the time zone. We spoke about surface stuff at first, but then I began to open up about how I really felt.

I was at this show with my nursing infant but without the rest of my family and was feeling really low. These were the days before Donnell and I toured together. I struggled with being away. Was it selfish of me to be out here performing? The other children were at home, and I was missing out on Easter preparations. I did not know how to place these feelings. I could not clearly see the balance.

"I should be home baking with them and teaching them things and doing crafts."

Frank replied, "Nonsense! Don't you second-guess what you're doing. Anyone can do dishes and crafts, that'll always be there. But what you are doing on stage is fantastic. Your kids will be better off for it."

What comfort this brought, hearing my father-in-law tell me it was okay to leave home, that what I was doing was a good thing, and it would all work out for the best. He was never one for fluff, and I trusted his conviction.

We often had meaningful discussions that still resonate with me today. Frank's exterior layers would unravel to expose a kind, humorous, passionate man with an approachable wisdom he loved to share. And share he did.

Frank's land and music and family are his living legacy. Never was there a more tangible witness of his love for these than his zeal. It was apparent to all. But even more apparent was the reverence he had for his wife. Julie was the pride of his heart, and he credited her for many of his successes. She is a radiant beauty, steadfast and full of love. They were an inspiring pair with their remarkable work ethic and many accomplishments. Getting to know Donnell's parents on a deeper level through the years was an honour.

When we had three young children in tow, Donnell and I decided to put more emphasis on staying closer to home and focus our travel on Canada and the United States. In 2010, we launched our first significant touring show, *Two Fiddles Two Pianos*, which included our very favourite pianists, Mac Morin and Erin Leahy, Donnell's extremely skilled younger sister. I loved this slick, musical powerhouse, and was so proud to be playing on stage beside Donnell Leahy night after night. However, in contrast to our expectations, amalgamating did not come easily.

A friend who knew our styles quite well admitted it was underwhelming the first time he watched us play a show together. Some people may think that fiddle music is fiddle music and that it's all pretty much the same, but there were significant stylistic differences despite our shared Celtic heritage. Donnell's fantastic technical athleticism was smothered by my steamroller rhythmic pulse, and my Cape Breton charm vanished under his dynamics. Our sound was, in a word, messy.

Then came the awkwardness — where to stand, when to talk, how to move alongside one another. I did not want to hog the stage nor did he. As leaders of our groups, we had worked to develop stage presence and a connection with the audience. Now that territory had to be shared, and we just did not know how to present ourselves while allowing the other to do the same.

Another element of this collaboration was our marriage. We couldn't just finish the gig and say goodbye until the next one. We had to carry around every detail of the shows and travel while we lived out married life. What to say if one did something the other didn't like, be it musically or creatively? Offstage, the endless aspects of everything from costume choices, set lists and material, venues, staging, catering, and interviews, and then on to recordings and visions for growth, became shared decisions with my husband. This was probably a more difficult learning curve for me than for Donnell because he had been touring with his siblings his whole life. No doubt there was a lot of give and take there. But in my musical space and touring life, nothing was ever shared. I made the call on everything.

Because our dedication to the music and our family consumed us, we were determined to make it work and work well. We had to. It didn't happen overnight, but we figured things out one trial at a time.

We both had to learn what made each other tick and what made each other ticked off! Mind you, we were never gruff types, but it was clear when something annoyed us. For example, I did not like when Donnell tuned his fiddle during my solos, and Donnell did not like my tardiness for sound check. I liked having a set list ready days or even weeks before a show, but Donnell did not like having a set list at all. Donnell detested existing in panic, while I could thrive in it. It became obvious that by learning and trying to accommodate each other's preferences, which was often easy enough to do, we could help thwart negativity on the road. It was of the utmost importance to keep the road life as enjoyable as possible for the sake of our band, our children, ourselves, and our marriage.

On the music front, our shared repertoire was vast, but playing those tunes did not work as well as playing new tunes we'd learned together. Co-writing worked better still, because we could craft sections to highlight our unique styles and create arrangements to showcase our individuality.

The most crucial change came as we listened more intently to each other while we played. I developed flexibility in my Cape Breton rhythm and adjusted my intensity to complement Donnell's delivery. New bowing techniques developed naturally, pulling more tone out of the instrument which was required when playing in unison. Listening attentively to Donnell while I played taught me how to allow the music to dictate what was needed.

Of course, Donnell had his share of evolution too. Through intentional listening to the overall dynamics within the melodies, he realized he needn't be full-on at every moment. He gained awareness of the intricate timing and rhythms within a tune and developed a subtle give-and-take in this new musical partnership.

With time and attention, our presentation on stage also seasoned. Not only did we combine into one sound, but our initial awkwardness was eventually replaced with confidence and assurance. That person who had first described the underwhelming experience of watching us play together came to our show a few years later and enthusiastically said it exceeded his expectations of what he hoped we might become. We had found our own little harmony. Performing with Donnell now feels like wearing an old slipper! Pure comfort.

Throughout our marriage, I have continued to work with a range of fantastic musicians and I fondly recall them all. In more recent years, three fellows have given us their best: Mark Kelso, Rémi Arsenault, and Elmer Ferrer. These bandmates bring their world-class skill and dedication to every performance, and I'm so proud they are a part of what we do.

Some of the delightful opportunities I hold dear to my heart include a Boston Pops television special with Michael McDonald, a TED Talk with Thomas Dolby, a featured track on Yo-Yo Ma's Grammy-winning album *Songs of Joy and Peace*, recording an original Gaelic song, "Woman of the House," with Rhiannon Giddens, DVD performances and a tour with Béla Fleck and the Flecktones, recording and touring with Johnny Reid, and collaborating with Darol Anger and the Nashville bluegrass community on *Blueprint*.

Most treasured, I produced a CD with Uncle Buddy. Occasions came along through the years where Buddy and I would play tunes together. I embraced every opportunity to play with him, for it required no effort on my part. He flowed like a steady river current and I only had to get on the raft to be carried along. His pulse and lilt were undeniable.

When Buddy was getting on in years, I realized it would be regrettable if no documentation existed of us playing fiddle together. I had an idea of recreating the magic of the cassettes from my youth and capturing it on modern studio equipment.

"Buddy, how 'bout we take all these old tunes you used to play and record them together?"

With his calm and gentle nature, he responded, "Well Natalie, I think that might be a pretty good idea."

It was easy to pick the material. I got almost all the tunes like "The King George Medley," "Iona House," and "The Bonnie Lass of Headlake" off an old Mabou Fire Hall recording. I can remember Buddy asking, "Are you sure I played that tune?" He'd forgotten a few, but we practiced up before the recording session and got his sister Betty Lou on piano and Dave MacIsaac on guitar to accompany us.

We recorded the CD at the home of Bob and Jennifer Quinn, Buddy's niece. They had a lovely home studio where we stayed and recorded for a couple of days while Jennifer made delicious meals. Genevieve Whalen, Buddy's sister and Jennifer's mother, came up for support, and my parents and Donnell joined in as well. It turned into a pretty special family event.

It all happened quite organically. Our original intention wasn't to make a commercial product. It was more for nostalgia. But after we had finished the recording, we felt pretty confident people would appreciate hearing those old tunes so we released our self-titled commercial recording. It means so much to me that we captured this music together before he passed.

Life rolled along with all the adjustments. Julia was born in January 2011, and was named in honour of Donnell's mother.

In Julia's youngest years, she was a mama's girl. Any time I had to leave the house without her, she was teary until I returned. She wanted me to hold her constantly, and we had this unique little snuggle. You know, she never got into trouble, and there was a stretch of time where Donnell and I thought she was darn near a perfect child. She had such an evenly balanced nature. It was about this age when Julia started telling knock-knock jokes. At one and a half, all she could say was, "Ma-ma, knaw-knaw?" Tiny little thing that she was.

Just a week after Julia was born, we moved into our new house. It had taken a year to build, and as exciting as this was and should have been, I must admit it was a strange feeling. Watching all these professionals working on our behalf, building with all new materials and installing entirely new appliances and furniture, weighed heavily on my conscience.

"How will we raise humble kids with all this newness around them?" I thought. "Did we build too much? Will they develop a false sense of who they are?"

I had been fretting even before we started the building process. My friend Leanne reminded me that beautiful things come from God and that our house should be savoured. When I told Dad my sentiments about the house he said,

"Don't be so foolish, Nat! You worked your little arse off for it, so enjoy it."

Well, we have enjoyed it for fourteen years now, and it has certainly become so well lived-in that I'm not seeing anything too new and grand anymore! Our kids never saw what I saw. It was just their house. Ironically, I am constantly doing things to spruce this place up.

In August of the following year, we welcomed a second son, Alec, who was named in honour of my father. As I got to know his personality, there were so many parallels with Michael. Alec was also very physical and full of energy. He too ran everywhere, even just to get a glass of milk. My boys would often play hockey in the basement, trashing the drywall with missed pucks. That got the newness out! There was actually a time when it crossed my mind that they might very well land in jail someday! This can be the way with rugged little farm boys.

We became quite the cumbersome travelling unit with five children age seven and under. But it was deep and rich and wonderfully wild as I continued performing about eighty shows a year. It wasn't any harder than the heavy touring days of my twenties, just a different hard. In fact, I've often thought about how those earlier years prepared me well for what was to come.

It has become a bit of a pattern for us, not waiting for life to pause as we figure things out. You know, that's one thing I've learned. If Donnell and I had waited for the "right time," I'm sure we would be without children. Life doesn't wait. It rolls and tumbles along, so it's best to dive in, figure it out as you go, and trust in purposeful love to guide you through the chaos. Years ago, I even came up with a philosophy: no time is a good time, so any time works!

Donnell has a confident, natural ability to parent, no doubt attained from being one of eleven siblings. He has always been awesome with kids, even before he had his own. He is great at making quick, sound decisions, and I have come to give his parenting intuitions more credibility than my own. He is wise and loving, with the goal of leading our family well on Earth and pointing our souls towards Heaven. The balance in our relationship has not only allowed for a peaceful marriage but an enjoyable one where our minds are clear and free to be in love.

While Donnell and I fortunately agree on most things, there are still times when we look at each other and wonder, "Where is the person I married?" Our annoying habits, cranky moments, and impatience surface through. Early marriage didn't have nearly the number of stresses or responsibilities as our life does now, and it's tough as hell to overcome imperfections with weights strapped on. When we're on different sides of a viewpoint and two or three of our older children weigh in with their views, you've got a quick tangle. Our personality quirks and weaknesses occasionally make for a bumpy ride. But we are able to say sorry when needed and continue trying to be better. We dive in again and move through the years and the mayhem as a team, adjusting as we go.

Reliably, love pulls at the spirit and every issue gets its fair attention. Sometimes it means we talk things out more and sometimes less. There are occasions when it's not necessary to have another opinion so I keep mine to myself, or times when Donnell just says, "You make the call, Nat." Occasionally, one of us has to just let go, which can be difficult if we both feel strongly about a matter.

Luckily, Donnell is, and has always been, a truly great listener. This is his habit. He understands me and profoundly cares about our family. I've found a freedom in trusting my husband's sensibilities, and I remind myself that the pressure of guiding our family doesn't lie on just one parent's shoulders. I liken marriage to the card game euchre. You play in pairs. Not all the responsibility falls on one person, and you can usually rely on your partner for a trick.

Humour and music have been our glue. I'm convinced that Donnell's sense of humour is one of the keys to our successful marriage and our positive home life. I look back at all the years now and thank God for it. Donnell brings lightness to our days with his comical sensibilities and refined attention to our individualities. He knows how to get a response out of each and every one of us. Even though we can predict his style or have heard the joke many times before, it never gets old. He is clever and his humour has strengthened our relationship and our family over the years. I find that it makes facing our challenges easier and helps me respond far more generously.

One of my favourite things at the end of a day is when Donnell and I sit in our two big chairs in front of our fireplace and watch on as the children have some free time to just be. We may have a drink in hand, or not. They might get up to a card game, some music, a great conversation, or silly antics. The struggles of the day are banished from our minds and we savour our home, our family, our marriage, and our life together.

When Mary Frances was three years old, I prayed that I would never have to homeschool. But it seems we live in the homeschooling capital of Canada! Many of my friends and sisters-in-law were homeschooling their children when Mary Frances was approaching school age. All I could think was, "Homeschool? Who has the extra time to do that? Not me!" The commitment, skills, organization, and headache — how would it even be possible? "Oh Lord," I prayed, "please don't ask me to homeschool."

In the fall of 2009, Mary Frances was eligible for junior kindergarten at a local school, but I felt she was just too young to send out the door. It wasn't really an option anyway because we toured four months of the school year. Still, I didn't want her to get behind, and I did have a teaching degree with a focus on early elementary education. I was curious, and thought, "I should pick up a schoolbook or two and just get her started on some basics."

So I asked my friend Catherine what she used to teach her children and where to find resources. I ordered a Saxon Math book and a copy of *Teach Your Child to Read in 100 Easy Lessons* and brought them on our tour bus that November. Mary Frances was a week away from her fourth birthday, Michael was two and a half, and little Clare was just a year old.

I got a kick out of it in the beginning, but it wasn't long before the novelty wore off. Getting Mary Frances' squirmy self to focus was a challenge. She had a rascally side to her if anyone ever did, and she knew full well how to push my buttons.

Every year it was the same story — there was no way I could put the kids in school with the amount of touring we were doing. Not unless I was prepared to leave them home, and there was no way I was going to do that. I'm not talking about a week here and there; we were often gone for a month at a time. Donnell was with me for some of these shows when he wasn't on tour with Leahy, but for many years it was just me with the baby, toddlers, the band, and a sitter.

I acquired more how-to books and read everything I could to try and improve my homeschooling abilities. All this research took up time I didn't have, but I squeezed out some moments, often late at night or early in the morning. The books stirred a hope in me that I could do it, and maybe do it well. I prepped from the vast resources I had collected and was excited to carry out my lesson plans.

On a smooth run, I'd start with an early morning rise, do a couple hours of housework, and then make a hot breakfast for all. School time would commence at nine o'clock with math, phonics, reading, writing, and religion. For the older kids, history and science were added into the mix. I'd have a fun snack planned out mid-session to perk everyone's energy, and then between noon and one o'clock we ate lunch that I had prepped the night before. Fiddle, piano, and dance lessons started for each child in the afternoon and lasted until about four or five.

After that came the kids' chore charts which included everything from food prep to setting the table, tidying the toy room, cleaning a bathroom, and doing the laundry. Then came a planned supper together at our kitchen table, after which Donnell either pulled out the cards to play games with the kids or told the most exciting made-up-on-the-spot stories that someday I will compile into another book.

I had built "five-minute moments" into my daily schedule sheet to allow time to answer an email or call Donnell regarding some decision that had to be made.

At the end of those nearly perfectly executed days, I would try to get some of my own practicing done, sometimes by playing the kids to sleep at their bedsides. I can't describe how rewarding it was when everything slotted into my daily schedule flowed as planned. I loved those special moments when a child really grasped a concept, got so excited for an activity we did, or had a musical breakthrough. Days like that provided the magic fuel I needed to continue homeschooling for the years I did.

But this sort of day was rare, and I was just pooped by the end of it. There were many unexpected events which threw off my allotted times, and I have to admit that I generally felt like a failure. Maintaining my ideal consistently was next to impossible. My scheduling was too rigid, and while I forced it through at times, I'm pretty sure no one liked me much on those days, which also made my teaching less effective.

I tried to learn the art of managing myself, to put on a good face. Inside, I was a screaming, crazy lady, consumed with her own timelines and agendas. Donnell could always spot the crazy lady underneath. But through the frustration and fatigue and effort, there was just something so gratifying about teaching my children. I actually loved it.

There were times I'd leave for a few days to do some shows and Donnell would take over the homeschooling. I carefully explained what I wanted to get done and wrote it all out for his reference. Hoping to see lessons finished and my checklist complete, I was always disappointed.

Donnell was well-intentioned, but he discovered that completing my list just wasn't realistic, especially given his many other responsibilities. He would inevitably take the children outside to help build a fence, clean the chicken coop, check calving cows, or go on some other farm adventure. He'd tell me, "I had them count fence rails."

Okay, I had to acknowledge that this kind of schooling was both healthy and a wonderful way to learn practical, real-life skills. Plus, the children were spending quality time with their father all while immersed in nature out in the fresh air. Surely these activities were as important as finishing a math lesson, provided the balance was right.

No matter what version of homeschooling unfolded in a day, they all carried varying degrees of success, and I eventually came to realize what many other seasoned homeschooling mothers had told me. Education is more about teaching your children how to learn and developing a love for learning than about *what* they're learning.

At the beginning of my journey, I think I focused too much on structure, curriculums, workbook completion, and ideal expectations rather than on developing a love for learning in them. I eventually came to accept the realities of our lifestyle and even embrace our unique circumstances, understanding my value as a homeschooling mom within them. I began to focus more on their achievements and less on my wish list. It was extremely hard to let go of what I hoped could be, but there were many other personalities involved and who's to say my way was best?

School mattered more as time went on, and Donnell and I had to ensure the children didn't fall short academically. My career also needed attention although luckily it sustained itself when I was having my babies. I started talking to friends about educational alternatives which led to a whole new array of solutions in the vast and wonderful world of homeschooling. These included various online academies, friends who taught courses locally, community and co-op programs, and lessons through video calls. They were all such beneficial options, but the greatest solution arose when a most special lady entered our lives.

I met Janet Shillinglaw at a friend's house one night. Donnell introduced her as his former babysitter. Revered as an exceptional educator in our local community, she had just retired after thirty-one years of teaching elementary school. One conversation led to another, and a few weeks later she came to our house to see if she'd be a good fit for our children. That was twelve years ago. Janet has been helping me homeschool ever since, and her role has adapted to the changing needs of the children and our circumstances. What an incredible relief she has been and continues to be. Janet is an excellent teacher and a marvellous human being.

Coming out of the pandemic, schools had begun opening up again before the music industry was in full swing. This meant we weren't travelling, and I realized that for the first time, our children could go to a brick-and-mortar school. I enrolled three of the older ones in a small private Catholic school. They were curious and eager to enter a new educational chapter.

I tend to be pretty cautious about sharing things Donnell and I have done to raise our children. What has been right for us isn't necessarily what's right for someone else. There are so many different factors to consider. Still, we've had time to analyze ways of doing things, and I've gained a healthy confidence on certain matters.

One thing I am pleased about is that all of our kids are quite appreciative. I believe that has come in part from not giving them too many choices in their earlier years. Instead of cooking only what they wanted to eat, we told them what they were eating. Instead of letting them choose what they wanted to wear, we told them what they were wearing, at least most of the time. As they get a little older, we slowly give them more opportunities to make their own choices. When they become teenagers, we allow them yet more opportunities to choose, and that's when it really matters. They appreciate we are letting them decide, which has yielded less rebellion and more gratitude. A grateful child is also less entitled, which contributes to a healthier state of mind. And the best spinoff? They openly seek our opinions as they enter adulthood.

When a child does not understand our guidance, I often remind them that Donnell and I love them more than anyone else on Earth and that they can take comfort in our love and trust in our years of acquired wisdom and life experiences. If they can't depend on us to guide them, who better can they depend on? I usually end by telling them that if we are wrong, we are not that wrong. Spoiler alert... this speech doesn't always work!

Developing a great work ethic in our children is high on the priority list for Donnell and me. We try to instill a mentality of working hard for what you earn, emphasizing that the more you put in, the more you get out. Failure should be used as a lesson so they comprehend its value. This is all balanced with the belief that life is good and anything is possible. We try to prepare them to deal with both big and small decisions, as well as to manage disappointments and responsibilities with grace.

I have learned not to underestimate the impact of positive reinforcement. While I don't see all the good they do, when I notice something I try to make a point of praising them. I can too easily fall into the trap of focusing just on areas that need improvement. They are great kids, and their light has illuminated my own shortcomings I need to work on.

We've also adopted a philosophy of keeping our children busy and interested in other things to help ward off the lure of phones. Having jobs for them, which happens easily on a farm, being part of a large family, nurturing special interests, playing organized and casual sports, learning instruments, and travelling with music have all been valuable efforts to reduce the enticement of screen time. Generally, age sixteen is when they get a phone. Homeschooling played a huge role in establishing a later age since our children were not usually around other children with devices.

Donnell and I may have a few things figured out, but I've eaten more than my fair share of humble pie over the years. I've been the mom to the only six-year-old not wearing pink tights on stage at the year-end recital because I didn't read the information sheet properly; I've been that girl dashing into the grocery store with no makeup, messy hair, and dishevelled clothes, hoping no one notices me, only to hear, "Hi, Natalie!"; I've been the wife wearing my husband's underwear because I didn't keep up with the laundry; I've been the mom walking into the fancy event looking poised and polished only to discover that my daughter has ketchup on her face and honey in her hair; I've been that mom who embarrasses her children because I've arrived late yet again; I've been the "professional musician" who somehow didn't learn the piece of music I'd asked everyone else to learn. Oh dear! Every time these embarrassing moments occur, I come face to face with my inadequacies and get knocked down a few pegs. While I hope each time will be the last, it's inevitably not. But despite my weaknesses and habits, I keep trying.

I've been fueled by so many great women around me who share a similar journey. They continue to be a great source of inspiration. We open up about our challenges and triumphs and I gain insight into other ways of doing things which spurs on positive change and rejuvenates my will. This perspective is crucial for me because otherwise, admiration can become distorted and cause feelings of inferiority and deflation. That does neither me nor any mother any good. We have children who depend on our positive energy for their peace of mind.

I always keep the powerful sentiments of St. Thérèse close at heart:

"The splendour of the rose and the whiteness of the lily do not rob the little violet of its scent nor the daisy of its simple charm. I realized that if every tiny flower wanted to be a rose, spring would lose its loveliness."

We all have a special place in this world, a role that no one else can fill. May it not take a lifetime to appreciate our worth.

(LEFT) Receiving the Order of Canada from Governor General Michaëlle Jean (and another baby in the belly).

(RIGHT) In studio with Yo-Yo Ma for his Grammy-winning collaborative recording, *Songs of Joy and Peace*.

Donnell and the boys check cattle.

Donnell and I practice at home.

A rare moment practicing by the stable on a beautiful day. No wonder it's rare… the dog wouldn't leave me alone.

Marking the addition of a new family member with a photo session in the field. (Rebekah Littlejohn Photography)

On the tour bus in the earlier days of travelling with the children.

The most wonderful Janet Shillinglaw by our front door before heading to the school room with Julia, Alec, and Clare.

Our first promotional photo after officially adding our children to the show.
(Rebekah Littlejohn Photography)

CHAPTER 6

The Family Number

Would you believe that the single thing I find most difficult is teaching my children music? In fact, it's the part of the day I most often dread! Sure, our children have always displayed natural musical inclinations from young ages, some earlier than others, but getting them to focus and practice has been like pulling teeth with every child, on every instrument, every day!

So why do it?

I often think that in the same way we must give our children good food for their bodies, we must also give them good food for their hearts and minds. With firm but loving guidance, we make sure they eat their veggies and learn their music, knowing it is good for them. With a natural capacity to understand melody and rhythm, why should we hold it back?

Donnell and I have lived the benefits of music on an intimate level. It taps into another layer of our humanity. When I am high on music, my mood is elevated and I become more open to recognizing and receiving beauty. Babies are cuter and chocolate is sweeter! Music has power beyond many things of the world, and we desire our children to have a deep connection with this lifelong companion.

We teach fiddle to all our children starting around age four or five, depending on their personality. Different approaches have worked for different children, but all of them have done well with Donnell's spirited, lighthearted, "keep it fun" philosophy. We also teach them to chord on the piano, and they receive theory and technical knowledge from Ingrid, a dedicated teacher with The Royal Conservatory of Music program.

As well, I start them on step dancing around the same age, but they eventually take lessons from local teachers or from each other. If you add some guitar and accordion for one, drums for another, singing for a couple more… well, it all adds up to a lot of music in a day.

I've tried simple schedules like:

2:00 fiddle
2:45 dance
3:15 piano
4:00 break
4:30 individual focus (singing, drums, guitar, accordion)

I've also tried some less precise versions like having them practice from one o'clock until five in the afternoon with a music rotation concept, which involved having a timer set with each child parked in a specific room to practice a specific instrument or discipline. When the alarm went off, they would all rotate into the next room with another instrument and the timer would be set again. This was tricky because Donnell or I needed to be there beside them to make sure they were practicing properly. It's hard to be in five places at once!

I remember running around from room to room for hours in the afternoons trying to check in on them, but it wasn't often that any of them got the attention required. I spent lots of time just looking for them! Somehow, they were out of their spot by the time I arrived for check-in. Apparently, they had already run through their entire list of practice material. Tireless negotiators they were! Ah, there was always something. And of course, with changing schedules, farm life, sporting events, and appointments, how could I have expected life to sit still while I perfectly executed my elaborate schemes?

Donnell's concept of just keeping the instrument in their hands usually ensured they went into practice with a good attitude, but some days were harder than others. Mary Frances resisted more than anyone. I could always see the music very alive in her, she just needed some techniques to release it. She was clever and had ways to avoid learning. Donnell persisted. He had a good gauge of knowing how much was too much and how much was not enough. I admired the love he clearly displayed through his patience with her.

When she was about thirteen, something changed. After nine years of cajoling, Mary Frances started practicing on her own. What? Impossible! She started to practice a lot, hours every day. To me, it was nothing short of a miracle. Not only did she practice, but she began writing and arranging as well, even discovering a love for Latin and jazz music! This dedication eventually led to the creation of her debut CD, *First Light*, which she released at eighteen and features all her own compositions. More importantly, discovering her capabilities has led to a life path for this dedicated and gifted girl. She thanks her dad for pushing her through those early years.

You know, I was somewhat like Mary Frances. I never wanted to practice in my youth. It was always a real drag, and I would rather have done anything else. But my mom made me practice every day. I'd ask to head over to the neighbour's house or watch something on TV, but Mom would first say, "Well, not until you've finished your practicing." Sometimes I'd hear, "That wasn't a very good practice. Maybe you'll do some more later."

If my mom hadn't pushed me, I would not have this cherished life of music and I probably wouldn't have met Donnell. As I see my daughter thriving now, I can't help but think of what might have happened if her dad hadn't pushed.

As a parent, you often have to work to get your kids to do things. After all, they need skills of some sort to survive in the world. They will at least have to know how to fight against the natural laziness that can set in so easily for any task in life. This is a hard fight. I remember it with my dad and my brothers too, particularly when he tried to get them to chop wood. He'd have to get pretty darn stern at times to see results.

It's a labour of love, this fight. It's never pleasant giving love of this kind. But it is love. I've received it. I've given it. I love my kids too much to allow them to go through life giving up before they've really tried. That won't get them far.

I'm glad we've had success in establishing practice patterns and habits in our children, but inevitably they will decide for themselves what role music will play in their lives. I'm confident that as they go on to explore their particular musical tastes, they'll discover, as I did, that their own heritage is authentically rich in beauty.

At fifty-three, I feel a responsibility to pass on my musical traditions. While I did not feel like that thirty years ago, I've come to treasure the connection to my culture. I believe it's part of my duty on Earth to not only create a good life for myself and my family but also to contribute in some way to my community and even to the community of all those who will come after me.

Now, you might be asking yourself how our kids made it onto the stage.

When Mary Frances was very young, we said we would never put her in the spotlight. No way. We were not going to subject her to our workplace. But look at us now! Before the children are able to talk, they are in front of an audience.

While we had beliefs about sheltering our kids from the public, we had started teaching music to Mary Frances. By the time she was four years old, she was learning piano chords, fiddle tunes, and dance steps. She practiced every day, we made sure of it. During our shows, she would sit side stage and just watch.

One night before going on, Mary Frances expressed interest in joining us but we said, "No, Mary Frances. That's not appropriate. You need to earn the stage."

Days and weeks and more shows went by, and Mary Frances was now pleading to perform. We held onto our views for quite a while, but ultimately it felt wrong to be so against the idea and we couldn't find a good enough reason to oppose her anymore. Our minds shifted, especially since she was continuing to practice. We were the ones who could afford her the opportunity. What harm could there be?

So up she went. Her first time on stage, she grabbed onto my leg and wouldn't let go. She was so timid, I'm sure it looked as if we forced her up there. The same thing happened on a second attempt, so we told Mary Frances that she just wouldn't be allowed on the stage. She couldn't go on hiding during a performance. She persisted, but we kept our word and held her back.

Eventually, the pressure built up again and we gave her another chance. On she went, this time hiding her eyes instead! But through it, she danced like a trouper. Once, she brought her new purse from Gramma on stage and used it to try and hide her face while dancing! Dear girl. She was so eager yet so frightened, but by the end of that year, she was playing her fiddle and dancing on stage. She was five at the time and off to the races.

Let's not forget little Michael, eagerly awaiting his turn in the limelight. He was eighteen months younger than Mary Frances and watched from the sidelines as his sister received thunderous applause. As you can probably imagine, he wanted a share in it too. This became a fantastic motivator for practice. We told him, "When you get this tune down REALLY well, then you can play it on stage!"

Over time, that pattern repeated with each child, until they all joined us on stage for what we still refer to as "The Family Number."

But the kids weren't always enthusiastic about performing. There were times when someone felt apprehensive about playing a certain piece, or a younger child would fall asleep, or someone was fevered, or had a sore foot, or was just tired of it all and disinterested. For the younger ones, we would let them rest while the other children went on. For the older ones, some of their concerns had to be addressed.

While Donnell and I encouraged them to try, we also expressed that they did not have to go out there. If they were injured or sick, we asked them to hold off making that determination early in the afternoon and instead wait until showtime to see how they felt. I would recount times I had been in the same boat myself years before. I was the only lead back then, and if I hadn't made it to the stage, the show would have been cancelled. It was through those times I learned I was strong enough to manage the challenges. I'd explain, "Performing shifts your mind's attention, then adrenaline kicks in and overrides the pain." I never had to cancel a show for sickness or discomfort.

Donnell had his real-life stories too, and we shared our little victories over the years and how we learned to work through the difficulties that come with life on the road. I don't recall any of our children taking the easy route in those circumstances. Whether it was to please us, to prove something to themselves, or not wanting to let their family down, we may never know, but they all rose to the challenge, and we made sure they knew how proud we were of them. I often perceived a kind of charitable bravery on their faces in those moments.

As touring life developed with our children, we tried to make the experience really great for them. We made sure to choose hotels with pools, and often headed somewhere exciting like a children's museum, a shopping mall, or an ice cream shop on days off. Between movies on the tour bus, after-show pizzas, and hours of cards and games, they always look forward to a tour.

For Donnell and me with our busy lives at home, touring has become a break. There's no garbage to take out, meals to cook, or recycling to sort. There's no farming, hockey, gymnastics, soccer, school events, or appointments. Touring creates time for our family to be together in rich ways.

When our children perform on stage, we are so proud of their efforts and know that our sacrifices were worth it. I see an inner vitality that's only drawn out by the music. As we watch them dance and play, struggles melt away and every corner of me is full.

I must admit I chuckle every time someone asks how I manage it all. The irony is that I'm always trying to find out how others manage it! I typically feel I'm only just getting by.

Most often, I exist in rush mode as I perform the duties of the day while thinking ahead. "Alec needs dinner before hockey, but I have to pick up the girls at piano, then get ready for the Zoom interview. I need to quickly fry this hamburger NOW before I pick up the girls because I'll need to leave with Alec as soon as I'm back, and don't forget that interview and then it'll be eight o'clock and no one will eat supper tonight if I don't hurry up and get this hamburger fried in the next five minutes. And if I can just get that load into the dryer — we are desperate for clean towels…" Then someone inevitably comes to me with their woes, looking for my attention.

There are no easy answers about how to remain patient and loving while meeting the varying needs of my family at the same time. While I can read and think and plan all I want, life hurls the panic, the rush, the duties, and the unexpected at me. Being patient is tough, especially when I'm in a rush. Sometimes I'm tempted to say to my kids, "Just do what you're told." A friend has inspired me to say instead, "Please, I don't have time right now to explain."

As a wife and mother, I greatly desire to create a place of refuge for my family. I want to make our house a stable home in which our children can dependably nourish all parts of their being. But how does one create this through the busyness of everyday life?

One of my most effective quotes for a quick recharge comes from Mother Teresa who said, "Every time you smile at someone, it is an action of love, a gift to that person, a beautiful thing." She has many great quotes about smiling.

When the kids come in from somewhere, I want them to see their happy mom. It's harder to show than you think. I am ALWAYS in the middle of something, trying to cram in ten tasks at once. Oftentimes, I have my head buried in a cupboard or my arms deep in dishwater, but I try to get a smile out when I can. It's a small but loving gesture to leave my own world for a moment and enter into theirs with a smile.

The role of cooking in my life has evolved. As children have come and grown, the importance of homemade meals is still near the top of the list, and we lived for years where we ate every meal together. I used to question, "How could a family not eat meals together? Like, how is that possible?" But I see it now. It's the same with praying together. We just do it whenever we can. If all of us are there, great, and if not, we do it anyway. As the kids have gotten older, sometimes getting together for a family meal means eating at nine o'clock at night.

There are many times when cooking is less about enjoyment and more about filling those empty bellies. Especially at the end of a busy day, the thought of cooking for our big family is sometimes daunting. Isn't the idea of making three meals a day for the rest of your life a bit overwhelming?

Cooking is an act of love, and good food nourishes home life on so many levels. While preparing food and serving meals may seem like insignificant tasks, these are the little things that matter.

For twelve years I have been making crepes every Sunday for brunch after Mass. No one tires of them, and if I dare make anything else, everyone is disappointed. I usually serve them with berries and bacon. And real maple syrup, of course!

One thing that I find works really well for our family is when I make breakfast for everybody. If we all get our own toast or bowl of cereal, we're scattered. It takes very little extra thought, but when I make something like smoothies and pancakes, homemade muffins, French toast, or my apple oatmeal dish, the kids get a bit excited and gather for a good fifteen minutes right when the meal is ready. Even that touch makes a difference and allows us to start our day together.

Teaching my children to cook has had immeasurable benefits and has been an enjoyable part of our homeschooling experience. This skill ensures there is always someone capable of feeding the family during daily activities. Oftentimes, on Friday mornings we have a group practice. They tend to be pretty purposeful sessions, like getting a piece ready for an occasion.

A few years ago, when older kids were doing most of the playing, young Alec had more time on his hands during the sessions. Lunch needed to be prepared, so Alec started making a homemade alfredo sauce which we've eaten almost every

Friday for the last five or six years. He was probably seven when he started. He'd peel and chop garlic and do all the prep on his own. He nailed it every time. I love the different sides of Alec. He brings his full energy to a challenge and has a "happy to help" kind of attitude in life.

"I'm pregnant! Again!"

In July 2013, I discovered I was expecting our sixth child. Donnell and I, although worn out, were giddy with the pride of having conceived another little human being. We were becoming a large family, beyond what we had imagined, especially considering that our first child wasn't born until I was thirty-three and Donnell was thirty-seven.

I had what I thought was a pretty similar pregnancy to all my previous ones. But at forty-one, I was well aware of the risks that come with age, so I entered a time of wondering about our baby's movements. Just as I experienced during all my other pregnancies, I imagined that our baby was not moving as much as is typical. Because this was a predictable paranoia for me, I tried not to pay it too much attention.

In April 2014, Donnell and I welcomed another beautiful baby girl into our family. After Daddy held her and Mommy got her snuggle, the medical staff brought her to the warming table. They discovered that her oxygen intake was low, but reassured us that she was okay. Then, moments later, our beloved Dr. Gow huddled with Donnell and me to quietly inform us, "Your baby has Down syndrome."

Hearing those words for the first time brought sorrow to our hearts. I can't dismiss the disappointment of receiving such a diagnosis. When I was wondering about those kicks, I had developed a confidence that God would give us another typical, healthy baby because surely He wanted us to continue making music and travelling with our children. It seemed so right.

"What now?" I wondered.

A couple minutes later, I said to Donnell, "She's exactly what we need."

Although I didn't really feel that to be true, I trusted it because of my faith.

My next thoughts were focused on Donnell. Although I could count on his love, dedication, and sense of duty, he was not made of stone. Would he be worried or anxious, maybe even embarrassed? And what about genetics? Would he wonder what caused this, whether her condition was due to his genes or mine? Could this put a strain on our relationship?

Extreme ideas can go through a person's mind when confronted with the unknown. I've experienced times where my heart and mind have gone into such a twist that I didn't know which way was up. But thoughts are just thoughts, and the ones that entered my mind when faced with this unexpected reality didn't need to be dwelled on. Perhaps they just needed to be thought before they could go away.

Love kicked in swiftly as I held my beautiful new daughter. "Natalie," I said to myself, "where is your faith? How terrible of you to think this way. You know this baby is a gift. You know the Lord Himself crafted her every detail. He chose you and Donnell to be her parents."

I really believed we were blessed. Now I really know we are blessed.

"Well Nat, we must get her on film like all the rest," Donnell said tenderly as he brought out the video camera to record her first little cries and cuddles. In the deepest part of my heart, I had a glorious moment of relief and gratitude for such a man.

As was our tradition, I got both my parents on the phone to tell them the news. "Well, we got a little girl..." I said, but had to cut Mom off before she began gushing too much, "and she has Down syndrome."

There was a brief silence, then Dad said in a most sincere voice, "Well Nat, I bet she'll be a dandy." This was the sweetest thing for me to hear from my dad. And he meant it.

Back at the warming table, nurses were still caring for our new baby, cleaning her, checking her oxygen, and monitoring other vital signs. But her levels weren't improving, and we decided to move her to the neonatal intensive care unit (NICU).

Our little baby was in trouble as she spent her first hours after birth on a machine. Of course, the staff was used to Down syndrome and the protocols for low oxygen in babies, but Donnell and I were not and wondered if she was even going to make it. Our ignorance made it a rough go for a while. We had so much to learn.

I was able to hold her and nurse periodically through that time. Latching was difficult and she wasn't taking in much milk, but I savoured every chance to pour love into this delicate baby girl. She needed to feel my love.

The next day, Dr. Jamieson sat us down and explained our daughter's condition. They had discovered a hole in her heart which was causing the loss of oxygen, and he talked about the possible need for surgery. I had heard of people being born with a hole in their heart before, but it was so life draining to hear this news about our own child.

When the doctor left, I cried. Donnell's face said it all. We were just so sad. There were no thoughts about music or travelling, nor of dreams and plans. This was beyond all those things. We could only think about our baby girl, her life, her wellbeing, and her journey. I wanted good things for her and felt a fire ignite within. She needed us and we would give her everything.

I stayed in the hospital while Donnell went back and forth to care for the rest of our children. Donnell was never one to open up with vulnerable thoughts, so I didn't know exactly what was going on in his mind throughout all of this. He told me days later he had a deep sense that God had intended the whole experience just for him so he would quickly learn to better appreciate his new daughter.

On day three, Dr. Jamieson came to tell us the plan. Our baby would get an echocardiogram in ten days so we could better see how her heart was functioning. After that, a determination would be made about how to proceed. He also told us that there was a small chance her heart might heal itself as she grew, but that she needed her oxygen levels monitored in the NICU for another day or two before going home.

Our daughter's oxygen intake improved and she was released from hospital the next day. The doctor's decision to allow her to go home gave me a boost of confidence that she was doing alright, that we were doing alright. Our stay at the NICU was four days in total, and now it was time to introduce this baby to her eagerly awaiting family.

When we drove up our long laneway, what a stunning sight to see our children waiting on the front steps, unable to spare the extra couple of seconds it would have taken for us to get into the house. This girl was absolutely smothered with affection, almost treacherously so, as each child clamoured to hold their new baby sister. Witnessing our children there together, deliriously celebrating their new sibling, with eyes only to see perfection, was one of the greatest things the world could have offered us.

Mary Frances was eight, Michael was six, Clare was five, Julia was three, and Alec was a year and a half. They didn't know about their sister's condition since we had decided not to tell them for the moment, trusting that a good time to share the information would present itself. I didn't think much more about it, although I imagined we would have that talk in a couple of years.

My state of elation was soon replaced with concern about our baby's breathing. I must have imagined her lips were turning blue because I rushed her back to the NICU. As it turned out, she was perfectly fine.

When day five came around, Donnell and I set ourselves to giving this baby a name. We decided on Sadie, after my paternal grandmother, and Agnes, after Donnell's paternal grandmother. Sadie Agnes Leahy, a fine and fitting name representing both sides of our family.

Later that day, Mary Frances and I were in the laundry room while she helped me with a bit of folding and unpacking. Out of the silence she blurted, "Mom, does our baby have Down syndrome?"

This caught me completely off guard. What could I say? I was not expecting this topic for at least another year. "Mary Frances, why would you ask?"

"Because you have all these pamphlets in your suitcase about it," she said.

"Yes, she does, Mary Frances! And that is why we are getting so many extra flowers and calls from people congratulating us. It is so rare and special to have a child like Sadie."

My darling Mary Frances smiled up at me.

"Sadie can't sin quite like the rest of us," I told her. "Sure, she'll be a little rascal here and there, but the way God made her, she just can't commit the same kind of evil. Your new baby sister is more pure than any of us." The words just flowed out of me, and Mary Frances was beaming a look of pride. I will never forget the genuine sweetness on her face.

A couple of days later, Donnell and I started a novena for Sadie's heart. During the prayers, I asked the Lord to heal the hole by Tuesday, the day of the cardiologist appointment, at which point Donnell declared, "That's ridiculous, Nat. You can't put a time limit on God!"

On the fifth and last day of the novena, a friend showed up at our house with a dozen white roses. You know what I was thinking. Two days later, we went for Sadie's examination. The doctor thoroughly checked out her heart, and with great confidence told us that it appeared to have healed itself and should never give her a problem. And it hasn't.

We don't think of Sadie as someone totally different but as someone the same with differences. She has taught us the richest lessons in love.

I remember being in the mall for the first time with Sadie. She was about two months old and had just woken up in her stroller, squirming and crying as babies do. I got her out, cuddled her in one arm, and drove the stroller with the other. I hoped people would see me with my new baby, and I recall trying not to smile because I didn't want to look like I was boasting. As I walked on through the mall, I eventually became aware of my pride… yes, I was proud of Sadie! I could never have imagined feeling this way when the doctor spoke the words, "Your baby has Down syndrome."

Loving Sadie is not something that I tried to do; it just happened. In that moment, I realized I was experiencing the gift of unconditional love. I loved her fully and for always, without expectation, without doubt, without criteria, and without a checklist. I loved her not because of how she made me proud or because she earned it or worked for it. I loved Sadie just because she was. She simply needed to be. That was everything. Sadie elevated my love so organically and effortlessly, provoking a growth spurt of maturity in me that has benefited our whole family.

Do you know the irony in it all? I had expected having a child with Down syndrome might prevent us from travelling and making music on stage. But Sadie loves the stage! She is the star. If you think I'm exaggerating, ask those who see her up there, smiling, fiddling, and dancing. She is full of stage presence, has the nicest bow hand in the family, and although she just pretends to play while up there with us, she learned "Twinkle, Twinkle, Little Star," at the same age I did.

My gosh, it's incredible for me to think back about my mindset when I expected to be giving up much of my touring life and career for the sake of motherhood. The opposite has happened; not only did I not have to give it up, but so many elements of my career have flourished! And our kids are a part of my music too, which has sprouted new growth and vitality, and has even led to their own musical development. Love always gives back more.

Sadie has always attended the school in our local community where she has access to many wonderful programs that suit her unique needs. Just recently, I dropped her off for the first day back after summer holidays. She was so excited, but then Sadie is like that every day she goes to school.

When we shared our usual goodbye, I walked away but noticed my smile lingered for several moments after. "Sadie pulls this out of me," I thought. "She has the power to extract a lasting moment of joy. I want to be like that for people. I want to be more like Sadie."

Eleven years have passed by quickly. I could never impart how special Sadie is to all of us. Her little heart, her adorable face, her triumphs and challenges, her infectious radiance, and her sour-stubborn-bad-mood-sad-side remind everyone she's just like the rest of us. These things and so many more are all Sadie. Her value in our family is irreplaceable.

I want to shout to the world how much I love Sadie. I want to tell everyone how awesome she is, how great it is to be her mom, how much we all love her, and how she brings out the best in us. I'm so proud of her and look forward to growing old with her.

If I had only lived my dreams, I would never have come to know Sadie. My husband and children would never have come to know her either. That would have been a tragedy. Life will never go exactly as we plan, and thank God for that. Dreams can be limiting, and I think we are made for more than our human minds can imagine. Love as nature allows and grace provides, and trust that the rest will fall into place.

Shortly after Sadie was born, Donnell and I figured that she would most likely be our last baby. We had lots of lovely children.

As time went on, I allowed myself to get a bit excited about moving past the childbearing years, despite the fact that all my girls prayed for another sibling EVERY SINGLE DAY! I reasoned that maybe that stage of life was over, with the exhaustion, workload, middle-of-the-night feedings, extra responsibilities, and restrictions.

But I also kept a part of my heart open for more. Giving our children another sibling would be the greatest gift ever. I imagined another little life to love, the bonding, the thrill, the vitality; it was such a bizarre balancing act since one outcome was so dramatically different from the other.

Who talks about this stuff? We were trying to figure it all out. I actually wrote a prayer, which Donnell and I said together daily, that ended with, "Lord, should we have another baby?"

In August 2017, I woke in a flash at five a.m., thoughts racing through my head, anxiety pushing onto my heart. In the isolation of the dark, I could feel panic pulsing through my whole body. Twice that night I had been roused by a bit of nausea.

"But… oh my God! Could I be? No way. But wait now…"

I started recalling other possible signs. If this was really it, I was not ready. But why was I worrying? What had I actually prepared myself for? I tried to internalize all of this as the minutes ticked on.

By six o'clock, Donnell was up and getting ready for the day. He could tell something was on my mind and asked me. I told him. He spoke very little but was not distant. I quickly drove to the pharmacy and sat in the parking lot, waiting for it to open at seven o'clock. I was their first customer. I was shaky. From the anticipation? From the fear? The excitement? I didn't even know what I should be hoping for.

After rushing home, I immediately showed Donnell the pregnancy test result which I couldn't look at myself. He confirmed I was indeed pregnant. Remaining very calm and steady, Donnell gave me probably the most memorable hug I've ever received from him. It said all I needed to know in a moment and was an incredible source of strength for me and for us.

I know this scenario is a light weight compared to the unexpected pregnancies that occur in far less ideal situations, but even so, we went through a lot of surprising emotions. I remember actually feeling embarrassed, worrying about what other people would think, that we would be seen as irresponsible for having yet another child, and me at forty-five. I felt shy just thinking about telling my parents, wondering if they might think the same. But my biggest concern was this child's health, given the complications that can come with age. It was such a bizarre experience and so dramatically different from my previous six pregnancies.

We slipped off to our chapel at some point that day and affirmed to one another that we needed to start getting out of these conflicted feelings and allow ourselves to get into a positive mindset. We decided it might be best to share the news with two very dear friends who were parents themselves and who had been wonderful to talk to about many things.

That night, the four of us had a most incredible and cathartic dinner at The Keg. After much good and deep conversation, our spirits lifted. We embraced this new little life, and I knew it was what my heart wanted all along. It just took a while to feel that truth. And that's okay.

Hands down, the greatest moment of my pregnancy was the day we told the rest of our children about the new baby. I knew it was going to be epic. Donnell and I actually set up the video camera to record this monumental announcement which we delivered to the kids through a guessing game. When Alec finally guessed, "Mom's having a baby," the children were beyond thrilled! There was dancing and screaming and smiles and laughter. It was just the best.

Our dear Maria was born in April 2018. We were running out of names at that point, but made our choice based on its timeless quality and how well it matched the vibe of her siblings.

Her childhood is going by like the pages in a calendar getting flipped far too quickly. When the rest of them were little, other parents would tell us, "Enjoy it while it lasts. It goes by so fast," and I'd be thinking, "Well, it seems to be taking forever! Would someone please learn to brush their own teeth!"

But having my little Maria now, I can see how quickly childhood passes by. I am making strong efforts to savour every moment. Somehow it's easier to do with seven children than it was with our first! Donnell and I are well used to the rhythms of life the little ones go through, and our older children are a continuous help with keeping the house running. They've developed little parenting habits and are much more stern than Donnell and me. Sometimes I find myself reminding them that Maria is my daughter, not theirs! No doubt they all have a significant role to play in her formation, but I often tell them, "Let ME be the mama!"

I remember going through customs one time at the airport with my family. When we approached the lady at the counter she said, "Wow, look at all the children! You have so many children! Why do you have so many children?"

I don't know why this came out of me, but I looked at her and said, "I still believe in love."

She went silent.

For many people, having such a large family would be scary. Well, it was for me too. I never thought we would have seven children. Sure, it was insanely challenging at times when we felt smothered by the overlapping, overwhelming responsibilities, but it was friggin' awesome! There was so much excitement, so much true joy, and so much richness. Witnessing my body do the things it was designed to do was miraculous. Despite my fears, it was thrilling to be pregnant, to give birth, to nurse an infant, and to mother all my precious children. Nothing compares.

I fulfilled my music obligations throughout each pregnancy, which on average was about seventy-five shows. For more than fifteen years I travelled with infants and toddlers, and I homeschooled them while on the road. Sure it was tough, but I wouldn't have had it any other way.

Why?

They are my children. I love them. I want to be with them and witness their growth in mind and body and soul. I want to tuck them in at night, greet them in the morning, take care of them when they are sick or sad, and delight in their joys. I want to be a part of their daily lives in a very intimate way.

I once read something from *Soul Gardening Journal* along the lines of, "May I go to the grave with rough hands, calloused feet, and deep wrinkles, rather than no laugh lines or signs of having lived a life of service." So, regardless of the exhaustion, it was well worth the effort and I am convinced it was a benefit to all of us.

While sustaining a musical career that fulfilled me, I was also able to provide my children with irreplaceable memories, foster their independent learning and musical growth, expose them to diverse life experiences, strengthen our family bonds, and toughen myself up in the process.

It amazes me how children who are raised in the same home by the same parents can have such different personalities. Our kids are no exception.

Mary Frances, nineteen, is the trailblazer. Her love of style has rubbed off on everyone, and she sets quite an example with her admirable work ethic. She loves adventure, exploring different cultures, and cooking. She is passionate and aspires to be a great musician. I see a wisdom beyond her years and am constantly moved by her humility.

Michael, eighteen, is now a man. There's not a day that goes by where he doesn't touch my heart with some little gesture as I witness the person he is becoming: confident, gentlemanly, hardworking, and sensible. The way he can make us all laugh reminds me of my brother David. Michael inherited his father's athletic inclinations and loves hockey and soccer. Farming comes naturally as well. He has a particular fondness and dedication to the guitar and accordion, and continues his fiddling and dancing.

Clare, sixteen, flourishes with curious creativity. From making homemade slime to dragon's beard candy, she has amazing focus for detail and often whiles away the hours drawing, painting, hairstyling, decorating cakes, and exploring other imaginative hobbies. She's quite athletic, enjoys gymnastics, and has a bunny farm which displays her love for animals. She's kind-hearted and fiercely loyal with an infectious spirit for life. She dances and plays both fiddle and piano, but seems to like singing best.

Julia, fourteen, is nicely independent. No more mama's girl! She is graceful, dutiful, organized, studious, and naturally desires to achieve. Julia enjoys horses, especially Ella, our pony. She is the most inventive babysitter of the bunch and gives generously of her time to the little ones, creating elaborate activities for them. She continues with the fiddle, the piano, and step dancing, but like Clare, she too seems to favour singing. Julia and Clare often get lumped together for many things even though they are two years apart, but as time goes on, they reveal just how different they are from one another.

Alec, thirteen, is a great conversationalist with his curious mind and insightful questions, and is a tough one to beat at cards. He is always eager to help, especially when farming with Donnell, and is sweetly empathetic towards younger children and the less fortunate. He is adaptable to any age from three to ninety-three. He strongly gravitates towards the drums and continues his fiddling and step dancing. He too has inherited his father's athleticism and loves soccer and hockey, although he might very well end up being the farmer in the family.

Sadie, eleven, is most certainly a dandy. When she is her perfect Sadie self, our whole family will attest that there is no one sweeter in all the world. Sadie is quite receptive to our direction and influence, has good manners, and is delightfully engaging. She loves her dolls and listening to music, and at times can spend hours acting out her own movies. She's quite impressive on the gymnastics bars, most likely due to Clare's influence, and totally loves playing soccer with her older brothers. Music lights her up as she dances, sings, plays piano, and fiddles in her own adorable way.

Maria is seven going on seventeen (an expression I never thought I'd use!). I don't know if it's being the youngest of seven that brings out such spunk, but she has a large personality. Inquisitive, sensitive in an endearing way, fun-loving, focused, and dynamic, she gets the most out of life. Every day we hear her eagerly ask, "Can I come?" She has started the fiddle, piano, dancing, and singing as well, but it's not yet clear where her greatest interests lie. It will be so fun to find out. She's a delightful little girl and we are all savouring her childhood.

Sometimes Maria crawls into bed with me and says, "Mama, make me warm."

I tell her, "Put your feet in my pocket."

Then I feel her cold little toes slide against my leg, and after a bit of wiggling and shifting to find the perfect spot, she breathes a sigh of contentment. This is my idea of a luxurious moment, some sweet, intimate pause where I experience the innocence and beauty of one of my children. And in those moments, I know with absolute conviction that I am exactly where I need to be.

Crepes

Total time: *1 hour and 10 minutes* ***Serves:*** *8*

While I serve crepes with bacon, fresh berries, and real maple syrup, they can be served with virtually anything.

INGREDIENTS

5 eggs
½ cup melted butter
2 tsp salt
4 cups all-purpose flour
4 cups milk
1 cup water

METHOD

1. In a bowl, mix together the eggs, butter, and salt with an electric mixer.
2. Add the flour and milk, alternating both 1 cup at a time and mixing well after each addition. Make sure to scrape the sides of the bowl to break up any clumps of flour.
3. Add the water and mix until smooth and creamy.
4. Pour a scoop of the batter into a buttered frying pan and create a nice circular shape by swirling slightly. (I use 4 frying pans to cook 4 crepes at a time.)
5. Cook over medium heat, flipping once, and adjust the temperature if necessary to avoid burning.
6. When each crepe is finished cooking, stack on a plate and cover with a fresh dish towel to keep warm until ready to serve.

Apple Oatmeal

Total time: *25 minutes*   *Serves:* *6*

INGREDIENTS

3 cups old-fashioned rolled oats
6 cups milk
¼ cup butter
¼ tsp salt
¼ cup brown sugar
¼ cup honey
1 tsp cinnamon
2 apples
¼ cup water

METHOD

1. Mix all ingredients, except the apples and water, in a pot and bring to a boil.
2. Reduce heat to medium and continue cooking until mixture thickens, about 5 minutes.
3. While thickening, peel the apples and cut into chunks. Boil in water until tender-crisp, about 5 minutes.
4. Serve the cooked oatmeal in bowls and top with the desired amount of softened apples.

Alec's Alfredo Sauce

Total time: *30 minutes*   *Serves:* *6*

INGREDIENTS

2 cloves garlic, chopped
1 tbsp butter
2 cups heavy whipping cream
4 oz. cream cheese
½ cup grated Parmesan
Salt and pepper to taste

METHOD

1. Fry the garlic in butter over medium heat until fragrant, about one minute.
2. Add the cream and bring to a gentle boil, stirring often.
3. Add both cheeses and continue a gentle boil, stirring until cream cheese is melted and sauce becomes thick and creamy, about 10 minutes.
4. Add salt and pepper to taste.
5. Serve over crusty garlic bread and pasta of your choice.

Chicken Pot Pie

Total time: 2 hours   *Serves: 8*

FILLING

INGREDIENTS

5 chicken breasts
1 large onion, chopped
2 tbsp oil, any kind
1 cup mushrooms, sliced
4 medium potatoes, cubed
5 carrots, chopped

METHOD

1. Boil chicken breasts in plenty of water until cooked through. Reserve the water and cut up the chicken into small chunks. Set aside.
2. In a skillet over medium-high heat, fry the onion in 1 tablespoon of oil for 3 minutes or until they start to brown. Reduce heat to medium and add the mushrooms, cooking for another 8 minutes. Transfer to a bowl.
3. Using the same skillet, add the other tablespoon of oil and fry the potatoes and carrots until tender crisp. Stir often to scrape the veggies off the bottom of the pan for an even fry.
4. While your vegetables are cooking, make your sauce.

SAUCE

INGREDIENTS

1 cup butter
1 cup flour
2 tsp salt
4 tsp chicken bouillon
6 cups reserved chicken water

METHOD

1. Melt the butter in a large pot over medium-low heat.
2. Stir in the flour, salt, and bouillon to make a paste.
3. Whisk in the chicken water 1 cup at a time to make a creamy sauce. If desired, add more salt or chicken bouillon to taste.
4. Add the chicken pieces and the fried vegetables into the sauce pot, stirring well to coat.
5. Pour the mixed ingredients into a 9x13 inch baking dish.

TOPPING

INGREDIENTS

1 sheet puff pastry

METHOD

1. Preheat oven to 375°F (190°C).
2. Roll out the sheet of puff pastry into an even rectangle and place it over the dish, covering the filling.
3. Bake for 40 minutes or follow the puff pastry manufacturer's instructions for bake temperature and time.

(RIGHT) Meet Maria! Introducing our children to a new sibling ranks as one of life's top experiences.

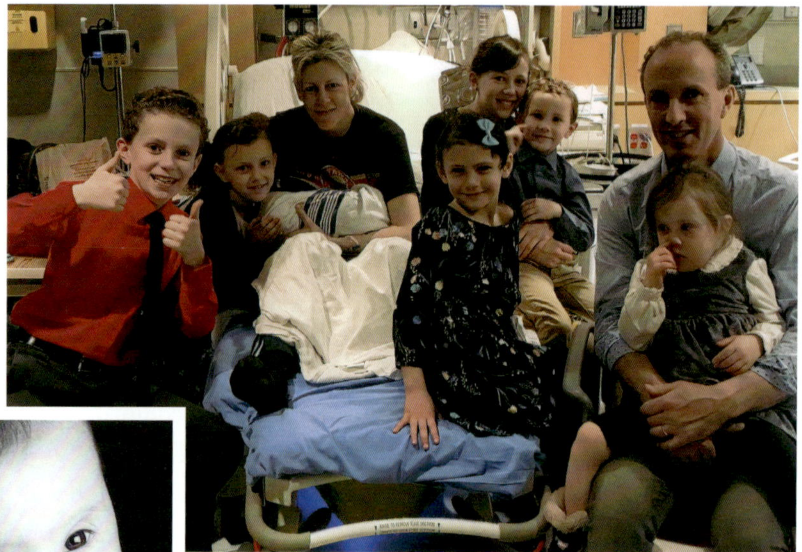

(BELOW) Sweet Sadie at six months old.

(RIGHT) Sadie and Maria sharing a hug on the porch after Julia adorned them with dresses, perfume, and lipstick!

(LEFT) Sadie becomes a proud big sister.

Mary Frances in her shy days.

Mary Frances excitedly receives the first copies of her debut recording, *First Light*.

Our Celtic Family Christmas promo shot. (Rebekah Littlejohn Photography)

An exhilarating moment as the audience, our family, and our band wrap up the 2024 Celtic Family Christmas tour at the National Arts Centre in Ottawa.

A candid shot of Mary Frances and me taken on a break during a photo shoot for Subaru.

CHAPTER 7

It All Comes Down to Love

In 2022, I received a phone call informing me that I would be honoured with the Order of Nova Scotia.

After hanging up the phone, I sat in our music room, alone. I contemplated the many times I had met people at the autograph table after a show who told me they were from Cape Breton, water filling their eyes as they shared the connection.

"How long since you've lived there?" I'd ask.

"Oh, it's been forty years."

"So long," I would think. I couldn't imagine.

Now here I was at my home in Ontario, staring out the window and thinking about the graveyard just down the road where Donnell, Sadie, and I had already purchased our plots beside Donnell's parents. "Twenty years..." I thought. "It's been a long time."

The Order of Nova Scotia struck a deep chord. To be acknowledged after twenty years as one of their own carried tender value, and my patriotic spirit swelled within. I love what Cape Breton put in me. Yes indeed, I am a Nova Scotia girl, a Cape Bretoner. You're damn right I am, and always will be.

I savoured this sense of pride while I sat there by myself, big tears streaming down my face. It was the first and only time an award made me cry.

Connecting to my roots has taken on more meaning as I age. In January 2024, Mary Frances and I were invited to join Galician piper Carlos Núñez at the Celtic Connections festival in Glasgow, Scotland. Twenty-five years had passed since my last performance at this festival. Mary Frances had just finished recording *First Light*, and at eighteen was thirsting for musical experiences beyond her parents' stage, while I anticipated seeing friends from my life before marriage and children.

As we made our descent into Scotland, I gazed out the window at the land that shaped my ancestors and the musical traditions I inherited. It had been an incredible life journey experienced through my instrument, and I gained a renewed appreciation for the insane touring life. Reflecting on the memories was like watching a rose blossom in slow motion.

The day after arriving, Mary Frances and I were seated at the Glasgow Royal Concert Hall while awaiting our turn to soundcheck. Karen Matheson and Donald Shaw were onstage ahead of us, running through the Gaelic song "Air teachd on Spàinn." Karen's voice was like liquid gold, shimmering, curving with the melody, and rich in tone. I had a moment of calm and just let the music pour in, its familiar pull tugging at my heart. Bishop Faber's words from our wedding homily, twenty-one years prior, came to mind…

"Two things in this world are eternal: music and love."

Here, the music had not ended. The music of my forebears did not die with them. Neither did their love. It was their love for the music that kept it alive, an inheritance which flowed through to their children and community, on to the next generations, then to my parents, then into my own hands, through to the hands of my children, and right onto the stage that evening.

As I introduced my daughter to the crowd, I contemplated the gift it was to take her back to the soil of our ancestors and unite with the other Celtic musicians on stage.

What would Maggie Ann, my grandmother, have thought of all this? In her ninetieth year she told me, "I wasn't rich enough to get a violin when I was young, but boy oh boy, if I had the money, I would be a violin player. I was alive with it." I'll never forget this sentiment nor the sincerity in her voice. Her connection ran deep and was beautifully visible, and I united with her love that night.

And what would Uncle Buddy have had to say? His passing at eighty-nine marked more than eight decades of fiddling and preserving the traditions. I recalled his many trips to Scotland to reconnect the Cape Breton fiddle style to its native soil, and his passion for the music and the communities who enjoyed it settled upon my heart. Buddy's dedication spoke volumes of his love, forever an inspiration to me.

I pondered Mary Frances' lineage and particularly her grandfather Frank. He lived a good eighty-six years before he passed, and I was so grateful to have known this man who supported me with unquestionable conviction and wisdom, fueled by our shared love for family and the fiddle. What he and Julie created together and nurtured with their lives would undoubtedly continue to have immeasurable effects on Mary Frances, their other grandchildren, and future generations.

Life is a fascinating journey. Sometimes, I sit on our front porch and pretend I'm a young girl again. I close my eyes and really put myself back in Cape Breton with Mom, Dad, and my brothers. After absorbing the memories, I imagine some mystical being whispering in my ear, "Open your eyes and see your life forty years from now..." Then I look around and freshly breathe in my surroundings.

"So, this is my home. I'm on a farm! Those are my horses? And there's a dog… two of them! I'm still playing the fiddle, and what adventures it has brought. Oh my gosh, I married Donnell Leahy of The Leahy Family! Look, we have children. I'm a mother! Whoa… and they all play fiddle! And my sweet parents are still so well…"

This exercise always fills me, gets me focused on the things I have, and pushes aside thoughts about the things I don't. While I hold in my heart countless longings I hope yet to fulfill, especially now with a large family, I believe it's essential that one takes time to acknowledge and appreciate what they have.

Of course, balancing career, faith, marriage, and motherhood can be tough sometimes. When I teeter too much one way or another, I start to worry I'm failing my family or falling short of my ideals. But the perfect is often the enemy of the good. I must step back to look at the greater goals beyond the details of the moment, recognize that I am but one part of a bigger picture, trust and let go, just a bit, and say, "It's good enough." And it usually is.

When turmoil hits, love isn't always visible. But it needn't disappear in the mess. Find it. I believe it is precisely in moments of trial that love can take on its most powerful form. It shows up when you make one small effort, perhaps in your tone of voice, or when you decide to really hear someone else instead of focusing on how to get your own point across. It could be in a smile, a kind word, or having a little extra patience. I know that God doesn't stop loving me when I've chosen to act wrongly, so neither should I stop loving those around me when things go wrong.

As we've faced life's challenges together, the relationship I share with my husband has deepened. Beyond loving Donnell, I like him and enjoy his company even more than I did when we were dating. I thank God every day for him and that we married for the right reasons which continue to prove their worth. That foundation has made for a joyful, fulfilling union and has fueled forgiveness and understanding in tougher times. Not perfectly, but enough to be effective.

And regardless of our faults, perhaps the most beautiful thing of all is that as the years continue, I know we are meant to grow even deeper together, renewing our faith in love and in each other.

Writing this book started with a trip to the grocery store seven years ago. While driving alone in my van, a rarity in those days, I thought about details from the phone call I'd had with Mom moments earlier regarding terrible news and suffering, right in Cape Breton. Then came to mind some of the horrific headlines Donnell had shared with me that morning before heading out the door. The darkness was suffocating and I became fearful for the future of my children.

Through the looming mental weight, I somehow forced a sharp turn towards positivity. I began pondering my children, the sweet details of their personalities, and Donnell and his devoted fatherhood. Intense feelings of gratitude burst forth in tears, and I thanked God aloud for the million ways love had filled my life. There, at forty-six, the realization came that I have a love story.

That discovery fueled in me a strong desire to bear witness to my encounters with love. Sorrow and heaviness can sometimes overshadow the hope and joy in our lives. I envisioned that if we all started throwing stones of love at this wall of darkness we could knock it down. Writing a book could be one of my little stones.

But I wondered if people would welcome my perspective on marriage, motherhood, faith, music, and tradition. My mind raced to the interview I had done early that morning where I had been asked, "Natalie, how do you balance career and motherhood?"

Every single interview I've done over the past nineteen years has come with some form of that question. People are curious. They want to know things.

In that moment of reflection, I was confronted by three realities: the interest of an engaged audience, the extreme evil in the world, and the love in my life. A conviction came over me, and when I arrived home, I eagerly started writing down beautiful memories. My thumbs couldn't keep up (yes, I've written this whole thing on an iPhone!) Over the next weeks, thoughts continued to pour out as I stole bits of time to document my experiences.

But as I wrote, my character flaws became glaringly obvious. I felt like a hypocrite at times, writing down all these sweet sentiments, then moments later acting impatiently with my family. I became uneasy about sharing my experiences from married life, knowing that it doesn't always work out for people. I understand why some folks don't believe in marriage, especially if they've experienced divorce. Life's harsh realities and misfortunes can destroy the best of intentions. I get it; even with a will of steel and a heart of gold, some plans don't work out.

Fear set in again and I couldn't help but think, "What if people figure I'm trying to sound like some Miss Know-It-All?" But through my doubts, the memories kept surfacing vigorously and I continued to write them down. Eventually, I chose to cast my fears aside and commit to the creation of this book, compiling my stories to bear witness to the power of love which can overcome and carry on through the generations.

Reflecting has been beautiful. I am profoundly indebted to Donnell and our children for their innumerable sacrifices which enabled me to share the stories contained within these pages.

And you have stories too. They reflect acts of giving and receiving love. Some may be grand and making headlines, and some the world may never know. These acts are your little stones, and they unite us in our shared humanity.

So, how do I balance career and motherhood?

Love.

Love is my guide.

I've gone through a million experiences only to realize that more new ones are just around every corner, each with its own particular spin; discerning how to proceed is not always clear. I'll never have it all figured out and I don't believe I'm supposed to. This is why love is the answer. Because even when I'm lost, I can always apply more love. It illuminates a path forward.

If there's one thought I could impart to you, dear reader, it's this: let your heart not stay idle, but relentlessly pursue a simple and extraordinary love.

Love is patient; love is kind;
love is not envious or boastful or arrogant or rude.
It does not insist on its own way; it is not irritable or resentful;
it does not rejoice in wrongdoing, but rejoices in the truth.
It bears all things, believes all things, hopes all things,
endures all things.
Love never ends. *1 Corinthians 13:4-8*

A view from our farm that elevates my mind and heart.

Mary Zita Payne
Photography
Home Cooking
Famous Daves
GET SAUCED
LEAHY
10

Acknowledgements

Thank you Donnell for your inexhaustible support and love.

Thank you Mary Frances, Michael, Clare, Julia, Alec, Sadie, and Maria for kindly and generously helping where needed.

Thank you John Serafini for your tireless dedication and incomparable generosity.

Thank you Jeff and Christina Cox and the MacIntyre Purcell Publishing team for your enthusiasm and hard work.

Thank you to the many people who have shown me love through the years.

Thank you good Lord for placing me in this tapestry of love.